TABLE OF CONTENTS

HOPE
NEVER
LOST

**A Collection of Five Mothers' Journeys
Through Their Children's Addiction**

Additional informational on Hope Never Lost may
be obtained at hopeneverlost5@gmail.com

Library of Congress Control Number: 2012923780
CreateSpace Independent Publishing Platform
North Charleston, South Carolina

We wish to dedicate this book to Diane Hurd,
the founder of SOS, who has been
our compassionate friend and listener.

God puts rainbows in the clouds so that each of us—
in the dreariest and most dreaded moments—
can see a possibility of hope.

~ Maya Angelou

Introduction

IT WAS FEBRUARY OF 2008 when I decided to call the number of a support group called SOS, Sunlight of the Spirit. Earlier, I had read about this group in our local paper and remembered saving the article. It described SOS as an organization offering education and support to anyone whose life had been impacted by adults or children suffering from addiction. In essence, it aimed at recovery for the family.

As a parent of a child struggling with addiction, I always kept a folder on my desk labeled "Lucy." Anything I read or heard of pertaining to addiction I saved in this folder for future reference and guidance. On that particular day, I was living in the midst of chaos resulting from my daughter's addiction. I went to the folder and looked through it for the number of the support group. I felt emotionally paralyzed with anxiety and fear and was at a loss for where to turn.

One thought prevailed: if I did not intervene within several days, my daughter might die.

When I called SOS, a very friendly woman answered the phone, informed me they were going to start a meeting in twenty minutes, and invited me to come and join them. l remember this day as the turning point in my struggle. For the first time I felt the freedom, without the shame, to openly discuss, in the comfort of others who totally understood, the sheer emotional hell I had been living for fourteen years. Over the next four years I found the ability to rise from living in fear and sadness to feeling hope and serenity.

During this time I attended the SOS meetings weekly. On several occasions our therapist, Jill, would half jokingly say, "You women should really write a book." Her words resonated with me. In the early years of my daughter's disease, I had so desperately searched for a book that would provide me with some encouragement. The thought of providing another parent with the hope I had gained for both my daughter and myself had become a driving force in my life.

One year ago, at the end of one of our meetings, I posed this question to the other mothers: "Would anyone be interested in sharing your journey with other parents?" The response from all, without hesitation, was yes. Each one of us at some point had felt compelled to share our story in the hope of helping someone else. This book is the result.

Hope Never Lost is a collection of five mothers' journeys through their sons' and daughters' addiction. The benefit of sharing with one another has become invaluable to us. With this in mind, we've set out to share what we've learned in order that other parents might relate and benefit. Our experiences and insights are spoken through our own voices and written in our own individual styles. Each chapter offers insight into noticeable behavior signals of adolescents starting down this destructive path, from the unexplainable changes in their actions to deception and denial. Too often denial takes over, not only in the mind of the child but also providing the easiest escape for the parent.

We want our readers to know that, although they experience isolation, they are not alone. We want them to recognize how we as parents remain silent for too long for the many reasons this book presents. Over time we lose hope not only for our child but also for our own existence. Our stories speak to our search for hope for our children while also finding hope for ourselves.

We share intimate details of the impact addiction has had on our family dynamics and the strength it took to move forward in a healthy way. We unveil our emotions, telling how we tried to keep hope alive while living in chaos. While describing our children's journeys, we also focus on our own experiences and how we felt as mothers. We talk about dealing with feelings, pulling the positives from the negatives. We cannot emphasize enough the importance of showing and feeling emotions. Each of us became active in family recovery programs and helped one another at different junctures in our journey.

These stories offer a unique portrayal of how we as mothers came to realize how we were enabling our children in an effort to help and protect them, how we tried everything in our power to prevent our children's self-destruction, and how we finally opened up to talk about it and seek help. Our words demonstrate that it is OK to talk about it, to trust what you are feeling, and to shift the focus onto healing yourself. We talk about how our child's addiction changed us and about the ways we learned to get out of the way and let life happen.

In addition to hope, the book sheds light on helping family members break through denial and deal with the here and now of how something is affecting them. It offers insight into dealing with a child whose behavior regarding the use of drugs or alcohol is concerning to you. It touches on acceptance, surrender, and forgiveness. Often, when one person in the family gets stuck, it can cause the entire family to get stuck in different ways.

Two therapists, Chris Wolf and Jill Fine, facilitated the SOS support group meetings and were instrumental in helping us as mothers come to know our individual struggles. They guided us in recognizing and transcending our codependence, and they share their wisdom through a balanced understanding of addiction in the last two chapters of the book. We mothers became forever grateful to these two women for their guidance and support.

As you will read in each chapter, when we changed, our children showed signs of change. This more than anything offered us hope.

Like a shepherd he feeds his flock;
in his arms he gathers the lambs,
carrying them in his bosom,
and leading the ewes with care.
Isaiah 40:11

JAY

EARLY SIGNS OF ADDICTION AND MY RATIONALIZATION

I REMEMBER THAT FIRST day when I realized that our son was truly using drugs. We were in a hospital room, waiting for blood test results. It was October of Jay's senior year. My husband and I had lived through several months of our son showing signs of drug abuse. But we didn't recognize these signs right away.

In the months preceding the hospital, Jay was able to cover up his marijuana use. He started smoking cigarettes, which we didn't like, but he followed our house rules with no real problems. As he progressed in his drug use, however, we started noticing some changes. He was not following our basic rules. We would ground him, talk with him, ground him again, take away the car; we would let him suffer the consequences if he broke the rules. He would follow along, and then things would fall apart again. He would say he was sorry and always have a "good" excuse for why he was late, why he "borrowed" money from my wallet, why his grades were falling, why he left school early.

I felt like I was going crazy. He would twist the truth and say, "Mom, that's not what you said…that's not what I meant." I always seemed to have the story wrong. The lying, the sneaking out at night, the missing money, the slipping grades, the skipping school, all of these things happened so gradually. We dealt with each situation and moved on. We kept thinking the behaviors we were seeing were him being a "teenager," that it was a phase.

Some signs of drug use are also signs of teenagers growing up and pushing back. We had two daughters five years and two years older than Jay, and we'd made it through their high-school years. What was the problem here? Why so much angst? Jay was a smart kid, very likable, kind and considerate. He was a regular kid. He was strong willed at times; he loved negotiating for what he wanted and was not happy when he did not get his way. He had friends in various social groups. He was athletic and played sports till high school, then switched to rollerblading and snowboarding. He had always been a daredevil so these suited his personality. Schoolwork had never been a struggle, but once high school came along he didn't want to put forth the effort to get good grades. Problems both at home and at school started.

Eventually, problems at school were happening weekly. Jay was pretty respectful during all of this. He was not one to swear or yell at us. He would complain and be frustrated, blame everyone else for his situation, get mad and go to his room. But he would mostly try to talk his way out of trouble. He could deny things so easily. "Just tell us the truth," we would say. He lied so easily. We all knew the truth, but he would deny it. What was happening to our son? What was happening to me? I fell for his stories many times. I wanted to believe him. I wanted to trust him. But I didn't. I constantly questioned him. I was afraid he wouldn't graduate; I was afraid he would get in big trouble at school. Our son was not following through on the things we expected of him. He was not responsible. Our relationship was one of distrust, disappointment, frustration, and fear. How could Jay do this to us? He was not brought up like this. Where was our child? I didn't know him anymore.

During this time, communication with my husband was stressed. We were trying to manage our son's behavior, but nothing was working. I didn't want to call my husband at work to bother him when a problem came up during the day—Jay didn't go to school; he went late to school; the car smelled like smoke; Jay didn't come home after school; the bank called me; I caught Jay in a lie, etc.—so I handled it. I held all of my angst in till my husband came home from work. I felt like I was the bearer of bad news all the time. I would hear my husband's disappointment, pain, and anger after I told him the day's events. He didn't want to hear all this. There were times when he just didn't want to know what went on.

My heart hurt. I felt alone. I didn't want this to come between us. My marriage was more important than all of this. My husband and I had differing opinions on things. He was more realistic, while I was more hopeful. Most times we were on the same page, but I was being bombarded with decisions. To calm my fears, I would call Jay to find out where he was, sometimes even driving to the school to see if his car was in the parking lot. I had become the police officer looking in his room for paraphernalia. I was the drug-test buyer, the first responder to bank problems and school problems. I was the one who found paper clips, dissembled pens, and rubber bands in the laundry. I was the one who got hang-up phone calls after he borrowed my phone. I was the one giving him money to pay kids back, to go bowling, to go to the movies. I was making quick decisions, believing they were good ones. I just wanted things to be normal. I was trying to find answers to this craziness, trying to keep my son accountable and to figure everything out before my husband got home. I didn't want him to worry or feel the consequences of Jay's behavior. I thought I could control all of this if I was vigilant enough and kept one step ahead. Where had I gone wrong? Maybe I wasn't strict enough; maybe Jay should be grounded his whole senior year! I couldn't stop the roller coaster. Jay was wearing me down. I wasn't controlling anybody or protecting anybody from this crazy daily drama. I was exhausted and didn't know it.

In October of Jay's senior year, we got a call from a concerned parent confirming our suspicions of drug use. We were done guessing. Was it only marijuana? We made a plan to wake Jay up on a Saturday morning and take him for blood work. Our doctor made the arrangements, and the testing would be done in the local hospital with results going to the doctor ASAP. Jay couldn't deny these tests, and neither could we. Jay was not a happy camper that morning. I was feeling scared and yet couldn't wait for the result of "just marijuana" in his bloodstream. I was still in denial that my son was an addict. I really thought he was going through a phase.

I couldn't believe I was sitting in the waiting room of the hospital for this reason. My stomach was in knots, but I was calm on the outside, sort of in a "just go with the flow" trance, as I look back. When the testing was done, Jay came out and said, "The nurse said I didn't look too bad, not like others he has seen."

Wow, that really helped my son's denial stay in place! Mine, too.

We got the results that evening, and the doctor set up a meeting with an addiction counselor the next morning, on a Sunday. Everyone came in especially for that meeting. Yes, there were drugs in Jay's system, and not just marijuana, but opiates. He didn't deny it, obviously, but said, "I don't do this all the time." I thought maybe he was not truly "hooked" and just experimenting. He could stop if he wanted to...right?

We developed a plan for all involved, setting up outpatient treatment for our son at a local drug and alcohol facility so that he could attend after school. Then the counselor stared at me, not my husband.

"Are you OK? You look fragile. I think you need to talk to someone about this."

That hurt me. Here I was trying my best to really be strong, and it hadn't worked. My physical appearance was telling the counselor that I was not OK. My mind was telling me, *I can handle this; I understand what is happening here; I know about addiction; keep moving forward...It's not the end of the world.* I really did feel calm, but perhaps it was because I wasn't letting myself feel anything.

I was sad, hurt, angry, disappointed in God, and disappointed in myself. But I didn't want to admit these emotions. If I did, then I would not be strong enough for everyone else. How could things have gotten to this point? What had I missed? Why had this happened to him, to us? Why hadn't all my prayers prevented this from happening? We really were trying to be good parents. Why hadn't Jay been protected from this, as I had prayed specifically through the years to keep my children from addiction?

I didn't even cry. I was numb, just going forward with the glass half full.

Now that I knew the problem, I could help Jay, better yet, there was a program to help Jay. This was hope.

BREAKING THROUGH MY DENIAL

FOR THE NEXT MONTH I visited with an addiction counselor. She let me tell my story and what I was going through. She always brought the focus back to me: how was *I* doing, what was *I* feeling? I felt hopeful that things would be OK.

After these few sessions, my life got back to normal, and I kept busy. I thought I understood my part and what I needed to do to help my son. Jay would go to OP, "just say no to drugs," get some counseling, go back to school, graduate, and all would be well. I didn't continue my sessions.

I was aware of addiction being a family disease, on both sides of our families. We had talked with our kids about addiction. When they were younger, we'd had to pull back from their grandfather because of his alcoholism; we had been part of an intervention for him. Some of our adult relatives were in recovery. I heard the struggles of these family members, and I could listen with compassion. But I felt our little family would not have to go through this because we were doing everything so that this would not happen. I could stop this. I was forewarned.

There was a lot of arrogance on my side of the street, as I have come to realize. I thought I could control these things from happening by being a "good parent." If I did everything right, it would turn out OK.

Part of breaking through my denial was opening up to others about what I was going through. Early on in Jay's struggles with addiction, my family did not open up to relatives or friends. We could handle it ourselves. When we finally got confirmation with the blood test, I shared what was happening with a couple of family members who had been in recovery for many years. We cried together. They were of great support to us. We also told some close friends who had known Jay since birth.

Deciding whom we could tell was also a process. I am very "loyal" to the family unit, which means don't talk about what other people are going through because it's not my business to tell. But by keeping that "loyalty," I was not allowing myself to be helped. Our son's addiction had affected the whole family. I was starting to realize I needed help. My life had become unmanageable, and it showed. I came to realize that if I wanted to start dealing with this honestly, some people in my life needed to know what I was going through. I needed support. I needed people I could talk to and trust.

Our two daughters were in college when Jay's addiction began to take hold. We kept them aware of some things, but not until the blood test did we talk more openly. They were just as much affected as we were, even though they were not living at home. What had happened to their brother? Who had he become? They also felt the confusion and pain of losing someone to addiction. They were questioning the things that they could have done to help Jay. Our family needed help to cope with this disease of addiction. This was the beginning of my recovery from the trauma addiction had caused in our family.

FIRST ATTEMPTS AT REHAB

AFTER THE BLOOD-TEST DRAMA, I took Jay to his OP three times a week after school. He was living at home and had lost his driving privileges. He was not eager to go. I had to be the one to take him, but that was OK because I was helping, not enabling...yay! There was a plan; I could help him. But actually, I became part of more drama as he began his OP program. Jay did not embrace his recovery plan…but I did. There were the random pee tests, the parent meetings, the calls from the counselors about him refusing to take his pee test, his all-around grumpiness about "this whole stupid OP that is not helping me at all and I don't belong there" attitude!

I felt exhausted and didn't want to be in charge of this. But who else would be there to support him? I never gave myself choices. I had to keep pushing him through, or I would fall apart. He had to graduate high school; he had to complete this program…right?

Eventually Jay was caught cheating on the pee test, and I was called to pick him up. My husband was working late and could not come with me. The counselor gave him and us an ultimatum: either Jay would go to an inpatient rehab, or he would be out on the street. My husband and I were so fed up by this time that we agreed with the counselor. I would take Jay a backpack full of his clothes for the rehab, and he would leave from there that night, to go to the rehab facility.

I was excited as I threw some things in Jay's pack. Yes, now we were getting somewhere! They had a bed for him…hope…answers. Surely Jay would go for that. Well, I was not prepared to handle the situation at the OP office. Jay did not want to go to the rehab. He would miss too much school. "I'm fine…I'll just quit…This is all craziness, Mom. I'm not an addict," etc. My heartstrings were being pulled all over the place. We meant business—he could see that, right? I couldn't leave him there to get put out on the street. Where would he go? How would he eat? There were a lot of crazy people out there just waiting to take advantage of this young, eighteen-year-old boy. Jay wasn't a street type of kid.

Fear was everywhere in me. Jay came home with me. I felt like such a disappointment. I felt like such a loser. I couldn't even follow through on a plan a professional had put together. If my husband had been there, could we have done it together? Why was I always the one? Why was this always happening? My mind understood that it would have been better to leave Jay there on the street outside the building, but my heart couldn't do it. Why hadn't I been strong enough? I was so weak. I'd helped cause all of this. I wasn't a strong enough parent his whole life. God was really disappointed in me. Those were my feelings, my truths at that moment. I held it all in for Jay's sake and for my husband's sake. They didn't need to see me upset; I didn't want them to worry about me. I knew we would get through this. But I wasn't taking care of myself. I was living on a rollercoaster of Jay's addiction. I cared more about his recovery than he did, and I put myself last. When I got home, I went to my room and cried, alone.

Fast-forward three months to February: We had seen some small successes mixed into more school-work problems, more lying, more broken promises, and more broken hearts. Jay finally came to us and said he wanted to go to rehab. He admitted he had a problem. Yes, this was hope—he was breaking through his denial. He entered the facility for two weeks, and when he came out he looked better. The counselor said another week would have probably been best, but he could go so he would not miss anymore school. He had to graduate, right? Just get him graduated—that was my motivation.

HELP FOR ME

IN APRIL I DECIDED to go back to counseling to get some help for myself. I felt so much doubt and pressure to make sure Jay was doing what he was supposed to do. So, during the next three months, I met weekly with a new addiction therapist closer to my house. She kept saying that *I* had to change. "Keep doing *your* life," she told me.

Well, I liked myself the way I was. Why did I have to change? I wasn't the one who was addicted to drugs. And I was still very active in my life. I wasn't staying at home and moping. But as the following story shows, I wasn't really living and enjoying things. I was focused solely on my son.

I remember going to a Friday night football game with friends. I was constantly watching for Jay to show up at the game rather than paying attention to the game. Then, when he came, I didn't want him to be there because I didn't trust anything he said. Just looking at him made me angry, kept me anxious. Then when he left, questions flooded my mind. *Is he using? Who is that kid he talked to? He better be home on time!* I was out, but I was not really there. My mind was in overdrive. I could smile and pretend, but the pressure was affecting who I was. I am sure there were times I wasn't totally present with my daughters or my husband, even though I really tried to be. I needed to change, or I would lose myself and not have a life.

I believed early on that my marriage was more important than my relationship with my son. If something were going to give, it wouldn't be my marriage. I didn't want this disease to come between us too. The disease of addiction wants to divide and conquer, and keep everyone in fear. It wants to close down communications. I wanted the tension between my husband and me to heal. I wanted to communicate better with him. My husband agreed. If that meant letting go of our son, then we wanted to learn how to do that with love. My husband and I were hurting, each in our own way. I knew I wanted to learn as much about this addiction as I could. My husband supported me in everything I was doing, but he had to find his own way to heal and recover from this disease. I wanted to respect his journey and not insist he do it my way. We were in this together, and that bond gave me hope.

I kept going to the therapist and listening. She said if I helped myself, it would help me find peace in living with a loved one who has the disease of addiction. If I took care of *me*, it would help my son. She suggested I go to Al-Anon and a weekly support group led by a counselor, at a place called SOS, with other people who were struggling with similar situations.

I went reluctantly to a couple of Al-Anon meetings, but I started to attend the SOS group once a week. I also wrote in a journal about my feelings, and I used my entries in my private sessions. It was a good reflection of my thoughts and beliefs. These actions helped me feel hopeful. It helped me cope. Through all of this I kept close to God. I never discarded my faith. But I sure questioned! My faith gave me the strength to keep searching for answers. This was hope.

When I began going to SOS meetings, I was upset by the stories I heard. They were heartbreaking, different than mine, but similar because we just wanted to help our loved ones. We all felt the same sorrows, the same fears, and the same helplessness. I didn't want to keep going back, but I listened to the counselor's advice. I wanted to learn how to cope better. I wasn't comfortable. I didn't talk very much. I didn't want to be disloyal. I wanted to put in my time and then leave. Everyone kept saying, "Keep coming back." Yuck! I stopped going during the summer. I gave myself a break! I did keep my therapist's phone number close at hand. And she was there when I needed her.

Jay graduated, but I could see the NA meetings slowly dissipating, and working his recovery plan became sporadic. Excuses abounded. The behaviors and rules he was to follow as part of a written "contract" that we all had agreed upon when Jay left the rehab facility, were breaking down.

I was feeling overwhelmed. I felt like my son was in second grade again, and I was teaching him about life in our house. There was no trust. I didn't *like* Jay. When would he get it? I was trying so hard to do my part, and to live my own life, too. I couldn't keep track of all these things. Life was unmanageable again. I still felt so much responsibility for Jay's disease. Was it my fault? If I could make sure he did all these things, he would be successful, right?

I didn't need all of this. I couldn't wait till he left for college summer school, and I was busy getting everything ready for that. He even said he would check into counseling at school. He was ready and excited to go. This would be where he would grow up and take on the world. Yes...hope.

He left, and I was free as a bird. I breathed a sigh of relief. I now realized how much my serenity was connected to his life.

Summer school did not go well, but Jay went back to school in the fall. Jay assured us he would do better, and I hoped he would. He got a job, and the first couple of weeks seemed to go smoothly. Then the money problems started. "Just twenty dollars more for the week...I get paid next week." "I have to buy something for school...we went out to eat." I would question, but usually put the money in the account. I felt anger, confusion, denial...I didn't want this to start all over again.

Then there was a roommate problem. I helped Jay move with some friends to another room. I knew something wasn't right, but this was his life; he had to handle it. I was not to get involved in his decisionmaking. More things happened and by the end of October, Jay had secretively traveled back to our home town to buy drugs over the weekend. He forgot that we were going to visit him at school and had to get back to his dorm before we arrived. He needed money to get a bus back to school, so he involved his aunt and uncle, who were not aware of his addiction problems, and asked them for money for a bus ride. They knew something did not sound right, and called us. The aunt and uncle made plans to meet Jay at a gas station to give him money, and unknown to Jay we pulled up in the car beside them. Busted! He was shocked.

We all went back to our house. It was quite calm. The relatives couldn't believe we had this going on with Jay. "Not your family!" They were more upset than I was. I had a different perspective now because I had opened up to change myself. I was talking confidently about Jay's problem and our situation. I saw addiction enter my house again, and I hated it.

I had been looking into some rehabs while Jay was at school. From all I was learning, he would be falling back into addiction again, and I wanted to be ready with answers. I was still doing the work, but it was for *my* serenity. We told Jay he had a choice of two rehabs. One was close to home, the other far away. The third option was to leave our house and fend for himself. There was not an option of going back to school. We were equipped now. We could handle this decision. We had opened up our life for others to be there and support us. We had loving professionals involved, a family doctor, and an addiction therapist. We had gained more knowledge and felt more confident in making this decision. Jay could hear it in our voices. I wasn't doing this all myself anymore. Things were not perfect, but it was progress for all, especially me. Hope.

Jay chose to go far away to California. I had been hoping for this. I wanted a true break from all of this drama, and I wanted to know he was safe. I put him on a plane on Halloween day. I drove him, waited till he used the bathroom before going through security, and watched to make sure he went through security—always vigilant, for his sake…for my sake. I found out later that he "used" in the bathroom before he left. I wasn't controlling anything.

For the next several months, I was open about my thoughts and feelings to two of my friends, who were counselors. They were there when I needed to talk. They understood. I think I went to a couple of Al-Anon meetings, but it wasn't a priority. I wasn't seeing my therapist or going to SOS. My husband and I kept in touch with Jay's rehab facility, but soon he needed to leave there to go to a halfway house. This meant more decisions, more angst, more complaining from Jay. We were helping him financially pay for the halfway house, so the questions were always there: *Am I enabling him? Why doesn't he find a job? Why is he moving to a different house? Why isn't he following what the rehab people suggested?*

Soon Jay was leaving the halfway house to move in with a friend for a month, and then wanted to come home. Should we let him? He didn't follow through on our original boundary, which was to be in a recovery program, get a job...etc. I was losing my confidence again. More decisions, more broken promises and hearts. Our relationship was dying. "It feels like you just wanted to get rid of me," Jay said to me. "I feel abandoned. Don't you want me?" Wow, truth in his heart perhaps, but I heard manipulation again. He was in the drama mode. I wasn't strong. I wanted to help; I wanted to see the good he had accomplished.

Perhaps this current problem was just something out of his control. I couldn't let him fend for himself in another part of the country. We could help him again here. We could help him get back on track at home. He was educated on addiction now. He just needed to get home and practice what he learned.

I felt like all these decisions were on me because I was the one going to counseling. I called my therapist, but she was not available, and I was given another number to call. This new person, Jill, was just what I needed. My biggest fear was doing the wrong thing. Would I be enabling Jay, keeping him in addiction? Yet I was the parent, and parents help in time of need. Jill gave me permission to love my son and pull back on a boundary I had set. Hope...a gentle voice from someone who understood addiction and the effects it has on family members.

RETURN TO SELF-FOCUS

IT WAS THE END of April, and Jay would be home soon. He had been gone for six months, and I hadn't seen a therapist or been to SOS since he graduated from highschool. I was struggling. I was handling this hurt, anger, and sorrow myself. People kept asking me if I'd lost weight. I am tall and weigh 130 pounds, so losing ten pounds did make a difference. I felt fine, but my body was telling me something different. It was very scary. For about two weeks, I could not eat. I wasn't hungry, and my stomach was upset. I took Tums and made myself eat something because I knew I didn't want to lose weight. In all my life this had never happened to me. I also began looking at things more negatively, "glass half empty". . I didn't like myself in this thought pattern. That wasn't me. I was not hopeful. I was losing myself.

I called the therapist and started sessions again. I started going to SOS every week and doing what they suggested to help me cope with my pain. Hope returned.

Jay arrived from out of state and got a job his first week back. He began seeing a doctor at the same time, someone who was overseeing his recovery. Jay was taking the drug Suboxone every day to help him with his recovery. He kept the job all summer and even paid us back some money he owed. He kept to his budget. We were keeping to the rules, and so was he. A few bumps, but things were going well. I had found my son again. He was working a recovery program. I had let go of controlling his every move. I was focused on my recovery.

In September I started having those bad feelings again. Jay was acting suspicious and making it sound like I was the one who was "over thinking" things. If you saw your child wearing long sleeves on a hot day, what would you think? Something just wasn't right.

I was anxious again. He did his own laundry, but I would find a bent paper clip on the floor or a rubber band in the dryer. It was always me finding these things. I was so tired of this. Why was I the police? I was being drawn back into the disease again. Even as I write this now, I can feel the frustration.

I contacted the doctor and told her of my suspicions. Jay was living in our house, so I still needed to enforce the boundaries. His door was open to his room and his backpack was on the bed. I hadn't been looking in his room for things. That was a practice I had given up. But this day I went in and opened up the pack. There were bags of needles, pieces of gauze, antiseptic wipes, a large rubber band, and a card that gave him permission to pick up clean needles from the local county health department.

I couldn't believe what I saw. This was truth. This meant heroin addiction. It was a jolt to my system to come face to face with the evidence. That was it. I called my husband at work, and we shared the disappointment. We both had agreed earlier that I would call him at work if something came up, to share the burden. It helped. There was no hurry on our part. I was anxious but not compelled into action. We would talk to Jay that night and tell him together what I'd found. We would come up with a plan **for us.**

I realized then that I could not stop this disease. Only Jay could. If he did not take responsibility for his addiction, it would kill him. End of story. End of his life here on earth. I had to let that sit in my mind. My son could die in our house just as easily as anywhere else. I was not controlling anything. Life had to play out. I could love and encourage, but I couldn't do his work. As much as I wanted it for Jay, he had to want it more. I had to accept the possibility of my son dying of this disease. That was the real truth, the real beginning, of letting my God take care of His son, Jay. He loves him as much as I do. He also loves me and understands my sorrow. I thought about this until my husband came home. I called someone in the program, and then I cried by myself with God.

We were calm when we told Jay what I had discovered. He was upset that I had looked into his things…oh well. Something had to change for me to be safe in my own home. I was hiding my purse, my jewelry, locking up our file cabinet, and always keeping an eye out so Jay would not go into our bedroom. This was no way to live. This was our home, our place to relax and feel safe. How quickly the situation had degenerated again.

We were finally ready for what everyone refers to as "tough love": kick him out. For me, this was not a "just do it" decision. It was a heavy decision to make. But it also wasn't like the last time, when I packed up his backpack and couldn't follow through with the action. And it wasn't like when he was in California, and we let him come home. I felt different. Through prayer and professional help, my husband and I were able to discern what was good for us. It was the right decision for us. I had learned that I could only do what I could do when I was ready. After going through this, I understood. The third time I was ready. Whatever I had learned from counseling and group therapy, it had given me the confidence to let go of my son.

We gave Jay one week to find somewhere to go, and we were not going to help in this endeavor. We had tried that before. It had to be his decision this time. He had to be responsible for himself. He could not stay in our house after the week was done. Of course, he was the model child after our talk.

I kept in touch with people who understood addiction and could support me through all of this. I felt strong, yet I was in sorrow over what was happening to our family. Would he be able to take on this responsibility? Would he be out on the street? Was he going to overdose? He was so young. There was self-doubt in my heart. I kept reflecting to find something I had missed in his life, thinking I could have stopped this from happening at all. Had I disappointed God? Most of the time, I understood that I did not cause Jay's addiction, but there was that constant movement in my mind to figure this out. I felt responsible.

I was also angry with Jay for not following the program, and I was in deep sorrow for myself, my husband, and our girls. My husband had grown up with an alcoholic dad he'd had to pull away from, and now his son had the disease, too. It wasn't fair. This shouldn't have been happening to us!

We called our daughters and told them the situation. Jay called them too, to complain: "I can't believe Mom and Dad are doing this." The girls were strong, even though they were going through their own emotions and doubts: "Jay, what would you expect Mom and Dad to do?"

Jay found a place to go while attending one of his NA meetings. He was to move in on a Friday, but it was not an easy move. A three-quarter house in the city said he could come there till they sent him to a rehab for detox and three weeks of inpatient therapy. The plan was for me to drive Jay down on a Thursday to visit the house and meet the director, then go back on Friday with all of his things. Well, after we got there things changed. The director talked with Jay and knew he was high, which I had surmised, too. Long story short, they found several bags of heroin on him.

Jay wanted to go home to get his pillow and clothes, but the director advised me to have him stay. They kept Jay in the other room as I talked with the director. I was praying the whole time. Here I was, by myself, having to make this decision…again! I knew in my heart that I needed to leave him there, but I didn't want to tell him face to face. So I wrote him a short note telling him we loved him and that we wanted him to get the help he needed. We would not be contacting him, and he couldn't come home. Then I left out the back door.

I was calm in my weakness, and I know God's angels were helping me through all of this. I wasn't confused about what I wanted to do. I was shaking, but I felt a relief. I had hope. I kept hearing all the things I had been taught in my head: *He needs to be responsible. He needs to take care of his disease. He needs help from those who understand the disease. God loves him as much as you do.* I felt Jay would be safe there, and this gave me comfort.

Looking back now, I see how this was a battle on another level of letting my son go. I immediately called my husband to relay the information. He was comforting me and acknowledging how hard that it must have been for me. Then a call from the three-quarter house interrupted us. I hadn't been gone ten minutes, and they were saying that Jay was going to call his aunt to come get him. He wasn't going to stay. They wanted me to get a hold of his aunt to tell her not to get him. She had helped him before with money and housing, and she would be concerned and would want to help him. She didn't understand why we made the decisions we did.

Why couldn't this be easier? Why was I always in the middle of this—making calls, explaining, etc. I was tired. I was spent. I was done. I was leaving everything up to God. If Jay left, I wouldn't answer the phone, if he ended up in jail, OK. If Jay died, it was in God's hands. Once again, I asked, God, *why does this keep coming back to me? Help me through this, Lord.*

Jay did stay that day. He did not call his aunt, and left for a rehab the next day. He got the help he needed and lived there for about five months. My prayers were answered in many ways that day.

MORE HELP FOR ME

AT THIS POINT I knew I would be OK, even though I wasn't sure about Jay. I had my family, my God, my group, and my therapist. They were all there for me.

Sometime that month I decided I wanted to get a sponsor to help me deal with this crazy drama of addiction. It had been suggested many times at meetings that having a sponsor to help you "work the steps" would help you move forward and recover. Months ago, when this had first been suggested, I'd felt like I had things under control. I didn't need to involve another outsider in our family business. If I'm honest, I didn't want someone telling me what to do. I didn't want to be talking about this stuff all the time. I was already seeing a therapist, going to a group once a week and some Al-Anon meetings every once in a while. I'd also found a friend in my group who was going through the same thing, and I connected with her in conversation outside the group. I didn't want someone else questioning me about things! It was *my* son; I could figure this out with my husband and therapist.

But after finding the needles, I decided that I might as well go for it all: get a sponsor, follow what was suggested, and hurry up and do these twelve steps. Then things would be better. I wanted to stop my part in this family disease. I didn't want to be a member of this "club" anymore. The sooner I did what they suggested, the sooner I would be on my way. So, I asked a woman I thought would be gentle with me and teach me. I wanted the serenity she had. She was so open and honest, and I wanted that too.

What I found in her was someone who gently stood by my side with no judgments. She was a friend who understood how mothers are affected by their children's addiction, and she was willing to share her experience, strength, and hope with me. I was finally willing to open up to that kind of help.

FAMILY HELP

WHILE JAY WAS IN rehab, my husband and I went to a seminar on, "How to Detach with Love." It was a good education for us. We were learning together how to respectfully pull back when our son was not in recovery. We learned more about the disease and how detaching helps everyone involved. More information gave me more hope.

In January I also asked my therapist if she would come to our house and explain to our extended family about the family disease of addiction and how we were trying to help Jay. There were cousins, aunts and uncles, and some neighbor friends. We also had relatives on the speakerphone so they could hear. We wanted everyone to know about our situation. No more secrets—we needed support, and we needed them to ask our therapist questions. We wanted her support when we told them our feelings, our story.

Jay knew we were having this meeting, and that everything was now out in the open. He would have family support when he was in recovery. Having this gathering of loved ones gave me hope.

In February our SOS group relocated. It was a beautiful place for us to have our weekly group meetings with one of our therapists, Jill or Chris. I was receiving support and no longer went to individual therapy. Whenever I chose, I could talk with someone who understood what addiction does to a family and how I could find hope in my life, even if my loved one did not get well. I would be OK. It took a lot of work on my part to open up and be honest with myself, but I was feeling better. I was learning about codependence and how it affected me. I was continuing my life. I was joyful again, and growing as a person; I could feel it inside. I wasn't feeling as sad or pressured to make decisions. I was glass-half-full again. I was finding me. I could breathe. More hope.

GROWTH

UP TO THIS POINT my husband and I had been helping Jay with rehabs and money. We were learning when to help and about enabling. I wanted so much not to be an enabler! I was learning when to detach and what that was all about. I didn't do it perfectly, but I did the best I could.

During the next three years I experienced times of sorrow and also times of joy. I had to cope with my fear of losing my son to this disease. I had to examine who my God was to me. What did God expect of me as a parent? What was my part in this disease? Those were *my* deep wounds.

One of the things I most struggled with was detaching with love but still feeling that I loved Jay. It felt like I had detached so much that I didn't even love my son. I "loved" him…but it didn't feel like it. All the distrust and lying just took it out of me. I prayed every day for him, but I was feeling sad because I didn't have those loving motherly feelings. Was I so hurt that they would not come back? Was I keeping them away? I knew I hated the disease but not my son. I felt sort of neutral at times. This was not a good feeling for me.

One day I was running the sweeper and I was feeling sad because of this. Had I really lost this connection with my son? I had been taught not to judge these feelings when they came, just look at them without judgment and feel the sadness.

That night I had a dream. A uniformed man and I were chasing after Jay to catch him. It wasn't that we were mad; we were just determined to catch him so we could help him. I was worried and scared; we had to get to him to save him. In the dream Jay was about eight years old and had a helmet on his head. When I caught up with him, I knocked off his helmet and he was crying. I asked, "Why are you doing this? Why don't you stop?" I held his head in my hands and looked him in the eyes. He said, "I am trying. I am really trying...I can't..." He kept weeping.

Right then, my heart was opened up. I felt like a mother again. I gathered the rest of his eight-year-old body into my arms and held him, and we wept together. It was a beautiful feeling. I did love Jay with all my heart. I wanted to stay in that dream. I needed to feel those feelings; they were a gift from God and an answer to all my questions. Forgiveness and healing take time.

HOPE

IN MARCH OF 2011 my son was in jail, and I was OK with that. I didn't run out and tell the world, but I told my friends. How had I gotten to the point of thinking it was OK for my son to be in jail? How could I be peaceful with that? How had I found hope in my life? How had I gotten to this place?

When I look back over these seven years, I can say with confidence that it was not just one thing that brought me to my current understanding. God, Al-Anon, group therapy, my therapist, my sponsor, my Catholic faith traditions, love and prayers from family and friends, and all those who shared their experience strength and hope with me moved me to the place I am today. Once I opened up my life to people who understood addiction, my life began to change. Once I opened my heart to understanding addiction, things changed. Once I gave up thinking I could control my son, things changed. Once I gave up believing it was my fault, things changed. Once I accepted that my son had a chronic disease and that he could die if he didn't take care of himself, things changed. Once I accepted that it was my son's choice to be in recovery, things changed. Once I accepted I needed to change some of my behaviors, I started to feel better. Once I accepted that God would take care of my son and loved him just as much as I did, things changed more quickly.

I got out of God's way. I let my son be responsible for his life. I walked in faith. I learned to take care of myself first, and as I did that, I felt better. I had more peace with daily decisions; I was not so hard on myself. I began to trust my feelings. These changes gave me hope. A big acceptance for me was the understanding that no matter what I said or did, enabled or didn't enable, I was powerless over my son's decision to seek recovery. That was between him and God.

I changed my fearful behaviors, not who I was. These changes came slowly with each month that went by. It wasn't easy. I discovered my own faults and how I could work on myself. I surrounded myself with people who lovingly suggested other ways to deal with my son. I had choices. No one ever told me what I had to do. Sometimes I wished they would. Ultimately how I wanted to relate to my son was always my decision.

I am around people who do not judge me and who accept me as I am. I have learned that journaling helps me to be real with my feelings and lessen my concerns. I have a "toolbox," as they say, of things that will keep me in truth and in serenity when addiction comes back into my life.

My history with this disease has shown me that the changes in my behavior did bring me joy again. My history helps me remember what addiction can do to me. It keeps me in truth. I can see that the choices I make now are not out of fear, and that working the twelve steps gives me serenity. The program of Al-Anon does work and gives me hope at each meeting. I do not want this disease to consume my life. I know that God, my family, my sponsor, and my

Al Anon community will be there for me. A daily search of God's will in my life keeps me moving forward. I don't do this recovery perfectly, but that's OK. Missteps give me an opportunity to grow, thank goodness. I still have sadness, grief, and angst at times when relating to my son, but I recognize these emotions and don't hide them. I feel very grateful for all I have been given. I have a full life whether my son is in recovery or not. And I love him dearly.

The disease of addiction will always be a part of our family. It is a part of this world. I am not afraid of it now. I am still amazed that I have gone from constant angst and sorrow to joy and optimism because I took the time to focus on myself and God's will for my life.

Recently I found an e-mail I'd sent to my counselor after my second session with her. I had written a prayer about my thoughts that day. This is a part of it:

> Lord, take away the sticks in my eyes. Help me to see my ways that are stopping me from being who you want me to be.

Seven years later I can say that this prayer has been answered. And only because God gave me the courage to take that first step and seek the help of others, to tackle this disease of addiction. As is said in the words of step two, "a Power greater than ourselves can restore us to sanity." God's Power remains my hope.

Today Jay is twenty-five years old. He has spent time in jail and has been in several rehabs. He has finished his eighteen-month probation period and currently resides in a sober living community. We are helping him financially as he gets on his feet. We have decided to do this, as he is held accountable for his recovery by his sober living house, which keeps us informed of Jay's progress. Jay is learning to take care of his disease and making his own decisions. We are in touch with Jay weekly and encourage him in his recovery. We are healing our relationship one day at a time.

Carol

May the God of hope fill you with all joy and peace in
believing, so that by the power of the Holy Spirit
you may abound in hope.
Romans 15:13

BILLY

CHILDHOOD

BILL AND I WERE married in 1980. We met in the neighborhood where we were both raised and began dating in high school. We did our fair share of drinking and drugs in our younger days but also worked full time, led responsible lives, and did not feel we were any different than other young adults our age. We met our friends in the evenings at the local bar, had picnics and parties, and enjoyed camping.

When I became pregnant with Billy, happy does not even capture how I felt. In looking back my feelings were of pure *joy*. He was the perfect baby boy and quite beautiful. I became a stay-at-home mom and loved the time we shared together. Billy's younger years were busy. He had twin brothers by age three and also a few toddler cousins. When they all got together, Billy was in his glory. He was the oldest, the leader, and always in charge.

In 1990 our family moved to a suburb of Pittsburgh, Pennsylvania. It now seems ironic. I was pregnant with our fourth son, and we'd moved to protect our children from the city. We knew that drug use was becoming more prevalent, and like all parents, we wanted for our children to be safe. I often wonder what would have happened to Billy had we stayed in the city. Would it have made any difference?

Billy was ten years old and the twins were six when we moved. It was difficult getting three boys ready for school while caring for a newborn. I remembered being pampered when I came home from the hospital with Billy and with the twins, but with our fourth there was no time for pampering. I had to quickly get back into the swing of everyday life. I will always wonder if I missed something in Billy, if I gave him enough attention at this time. Sometimes birth order can play a role in personality. Did I expect too much or not enough?

In 1996 the owner of my husband's company died, and to our disbelief, he left the company to my husband. For the first time in our lives we saw a light at the end of our tunnel of debt. My husband came home one night with the will and read it to us. We were so hopeful for our children's future. We could help them with sporting activities, college, and everything in between.

THE ONSET OF ADDICTIVE BEHAVIOR

THE FEELINGS OF BETRAYAL really don't begin to touch the surface when it comes to addiction. My husband and I were so naïve and just plain blindsided by Billy's addiction. It started in high school with drinking at football games and lots of sleepovers. Some families would let the kids drink at their homes and take the car keys. For most kids drinking is no problem, but I say you never know when addiction becomes fully active and takes over your being. Billy's first arrest for alcohol was at a football game. I remember driving to the police station to get him. My husband and I were crying and laughing. Don't get me wrong: we were very upset and anxious, but we had also been arrested when we were seventeen for underage drinking. For Billy, however, this was the beginning of cutting school, repeating the eleventh grade, and finally taking his GED. Billy had a way of making you believe that he would be able to get through his classes and make it to his senior year. He always thought he would be able to pull everything together. We were the ones to tell him that he wasn't repeating the eleventh grade for the third time. He finally agreed and took his GED.

Billy began to work at a local gas station, where he was getting high and not coming home. His behavior had started to get out of hand. We were never very sure if it was drinking or something else. All I knew was that things in his life just did not add up. That Christmas Eve, as we did every year since I can remember, we got together with the whole family. Billy and his twin brothers drove together in one car. When they arrived, we noticed that Billy was very high. I'm still not sure what he was on that night, but whatever it was, my father noticed. The day after Christmas, my father went to the gas station to question Billy, who said everything was fine: "Don't worry, Pap." But Pap was worried and called me with his concerns. After the conversation with my father, I went to Billy's room. As I was walking toward it, I remember praying for God's help.

This is the part that I found so difficult to believe: in Billy's closet I found a present his brother bought him from the Santa Store at school. It was one of those plastic banks shaped like a dollar bill, and the top could be easily removed. Inside the bank were little blue bags with Mickey Mouse stamped on them. I called my husband and then my sister. They both knew it was heroin. I asked my husband to come home and asked my sister to come over. I also called my parents and my older sister. My husband picked up Billy from work, and we had a family intervention. Billy confessed, and the next day we placed him in a rehab facility for ten days, the time our insurance would pay. If I had known then, what I know now, I would have found a way to pay for him to stay at least six months.

Rehab and Consequences

THAT WAS THE BEGINNING of many attempts at rehabs: Gateway, Greenbrier, Freedom House, Braddock Hospital, Glenbeigh, and then finally jail. It has been twelve years now since Billy exhibited the first signs of addiction. As I recall everything that we went through, I sometimes can't believe how it took over our lives. I remember going to an eighth-grade carnival with the twins. I was with another mother whose son had just been accepted into one of the best colleges. *Where had we gone wrong?* I asked myself. We just wanted our son to get his GED.

In September of 2004 one of our twins was diagnosed with leukemia (CML). When Billy found out, he relapsed again. I had a son with leukemia and a month later another son in rehab. My world fell apart. I felt so alone, sad, frightened, and empty. It was difficult to leave my house. If I saw anyone I knew at the grocery store, I turned the other way. I visited our pastor and told him that I had lost my joy. I was so broken inside that I could not even do simple, happy things, like walk my puppy or hold my neighbor's baby.

The following day I accepted my neighbor's invitation to go shopping. We were on our way home when her six-month-old began crying. As I reached around to hold the bottle for him, I noticed the license plate on the car behind us. It simply read JOY; I was speechless. The following night, I woke up with the realization that the license plate was a sign that I was going to be OK. It was the word, the sign, the faith that *Jesus Offers You:* JOY. I came to realize what I was missing: I needed my inner joy that I had lost through this awful storm. I often talk about how much my faith has grown from this experience. If I have learned anything, it is to trust God and to lean on Him as a great comforter.

After many rehabs, Billy decided to go to a methadone clinic as the counselor at his last rehab had suggested. This is so hard for me to write about: I believe that methadone is pure poison, and the money made from it is unbelievable. I know now that Billy was still getting high from eighty milligrams of methadone. Shortly after he started the program, he learned from others in treatment that mixing Xanax with the methadone creates almost the same high as heroin. This combination of drugs is also very deadly. I watched Billy gain one hundred pounds, from 150 to 250. He was able to hold a job during this time, but when he came home he just slept. He was like a zombie.

One night I was paying bills and noticed a $254 withdrawal from my account. Billy denied knowing anything about it. I contacted the freight company listed on my bank statement and learned that ninety Xanax pills had been delivered to our address. The phone number on the order belonged to my son. Billy had ordered the pills from an online doctor in England. My husband and I demanded the pills, but of course,

Billy could not remember where they were. We went to bed that night exhausted from this nightmare. As I woke the following morning, I remember thinking that Billy could be dead from an overdose. And I remember saying to God, "That would be all right." Could the pain of losing a child be any worse than the anguish of seeing him slowly kill himself?

HELP FOR MYSELF

AT THIS POINT I recognized how much I needed help. This was no longer just Billy's addiction. I had become his enabler. I began to attend Al-Anon meetings and found a group called The Sunlight of the Spirit (SOS). At my first meeting I told everyone about my words to God, about it being all right if Billy died. The therapist stopped the meeting and asked everyone if they ever felt this way. Everyone raised his or her hands. I knew I was in the right place. It took time, but slowly I no longer blamed myself for Billy's drug use. I made him accountable for his own money and bills. I informed his local doctor about his combining the methadone and Xanax.

I started the process of taking charge of my life and letting go of Billy's. In one of our SOS sessions, we talked about ladders. In the room against one of the walls were two ladders, each with a stuffed animal on one of the steps. This gave me the visual I needed and still use today. I WAS TO STAY ON MY OWN LADDER. The wheels were in motion, and I had to use my faith in God to let go.

One morning that month, I noticed that Billy was very agitated as he was getting ready to go to work. He was out of Xanax, had no money, and appeared to be desperate. A few hours later, I left to walk our dog, and when I returned, the police were at our house. Billy had gone to the drug store, gone behind the pharmacy counter, and stolen three large bottles of Xanax. He had pulled his shirt up over his mouth and was carrying what he called a box knife. Luckily he did not hurt anyone.

Billy spent three weeks in jail. I was very worried about him, but I was also embarrassed by what he had done. I didn't want to tell anyone, but I had to call my parents and my sisters. Billy knew their phone numbers, and I was worried that he would call them to bail him out. The last thing I wanted was for him to come home or go to my parents' home. Billy's arrest was awful, but the upside was that he did not receive any methadone or Xanax in jail. At the end of the three weeks, the magistrate agreed to send him to a rehab facility outside of Cleveland, where he stayed for a year. Afterward, he found an apartment and worked at a pizza shop. We later learned his neighbor sold drugs, and by the time of his final court hearing, Billy was using again. I could see the sweating and flu-like symptoms, and I truly believed he was sick. He was, but not with the flu. At the hearing the judge gave him five years probation.

This time Billy went on a drug called Suboxone to withdraw from heroin. Before long he was drinking heavily and received two DUIs. He was sentenced to go to jail on weekends for one DUI, as during the week he was working for a landscape company. In July 2010 he had a seizure and was hospitalized for three days. He missed his weekend in jail, which resulted in a warrant for his arrest. A police officer pulled Billy over after he had purchased drugs, this time cocaine, and recognized his name as being wanted. Billy landed in jail for another year.

My husband and I visited him every other week. We chose not to get an attorney and instead went with a public defender because we were still in debt for Billy's rehab in Cleveland. Some decisions are not easy to make, but we were also paying for his phone privileges and placing money on his books so he could buy essentials. Having a son in jail is never easy, but when I went to bed at night, I knew he was safe. This was the only time I was certain he was alive, clean, and sober.

CONCLUSION

Billy was released from jail in August 2011. He is working for his father and living with his girlfriend. They have two dogs and a kitten. I wish I could write about a happy ending here, but Billy's story is not over. Every day I pray for him to recognize how God works in our lives. He saved Billy the first time from the methadone and Xanax combination and the second time from cocaine. It was only a matter of time before cocaine would become his next drug of choice.

I have learned to take care of myself. I know that I will always have my joy. I know that from time to time I will try to climb Billy's ladder. It is at these times that I will apply what I have learned: call my sponsor, go to support group meetings, and analyze where mother ends and enabler begins. I will always be thankful to the SOS group for showing me how to survive Billy's addiction and, most importantly, how to love my son in good times and in bad.

Our son with leukemia is doing very well. His physician expects him to live a very full life. I find myself on his ladder sometimes, but with the tools I have learned I know I can let go and let God. I wish to give thanks to:

God,

My family for going to family counseling sessions,

My husband for listening to all that I have learned from SOS,

Chris Wolf and Jill Fine for their knowledge and guidance,

My friend for listening to my worries and having the courage to tell me I needed help, and

My pastor for always being there for me when I had no where to turn.

Sandy

Hope, like the gleaming taper's light
Adorns and cheers our ray;
And still, as darker grows the night,
Emits a lighter ray.
Oliver Goldmith

LUCY

CHILDHOOD

LUCY WAS THE YOUNGER of two children, born seven years after the birth of her sister, Lisa. As a child she appeared to be happy most of the time with a sweet and sensitive disposition. I remember her third-grade teacher, who was also her kindergarten teacher, telling me one day that Lucy got along with everyone and all the girls in the class gravitated around her. Her pre-kindergarten testing indicated that she was somewhat behind in her numbers and alphabet, but it did not appear to be a major concern. However, several years later in third grade, her teacher recommended that she be privately tutored in reading. We found a local teacher who remained as Lucy's tutor once a week through her junior year of high school, and in the ninth grade Lucy was diagnosed as having ADD and was prescribed Ritalin.

She took dance lessons from age four to age twelve and was a youth cheerleader through the seventh grade. She enjoyed learning to do things with her hands especially pottery, knitting and sewing, and began using the sewing machine in grade school. Until Lisa left home to go to college, when Lucy was ten, Lucy would normally prevail when there was a conflict between she and her sister. I now realize that Lucy's father and I unintentionally allowed this to happen. But I believe we did this for two reasons: one, Lucy was always the most difficult to reason with, and two, Lisa was the oldest, and therefore higher expectations were set. Also, Lisa was a precocious child and more mature for her age. As a result Lucy was not only the baby of the family chronologically but was also babied by the family around her.

Between the age of ten and twelve, Lucy gained some weight and became very self-conscious about her appearance, always complaining about looking fat. It was from this point on that her low self-esteem and insecurity became apparent.

I strongly believe low self-esteem at this age can contribute to addiction issues later. I also believe the frustration ADD can create predisposes young adults to engage in substance abuse. The third factor that cannot be ignored is heredity, which I believe could also have contributed to Lucy's addiction.

When her father and I first met, I was not only attracted to his kindness and compassion but to his outgoing and fun-loving nature. We dated for nine months prior to our marriage. During this period of time, I became concerned about too much "fun loving" but felt that would change in time. As a wise older gentleman had once told me, "Don't ever marry someone thinking you will change them after you take your vows," but that is exactly what I did; and our daughters had to endure the turmoil it created throughout our twenty-eight years of marriage. I was constantly trying to change my husband's behavior while he saw no need to change, nor did he have any desire to do so. We were both wrong, I for my persistence and he for lack of willingness. Although he struggled with addictive behavior, he was a very openly loving, caring and lighthearted father who added much laughter and happiness to the family. He provided loving guidance to Lisa and Lucy through very solid advice. In disciplinary matters, he took somewhat of a back seat, leaving most of the important decisions surrounding consequences up to me. He was always very supportive of the actions taken, but neither one of us could have ever been prepared for the challenge that lay ahead.

High-School Years

IT WAS JANUARY 16, 1994, Lucy's fourteenth birthday. She had invited two of her closest friends to our home that Friday for a sleepover. The next day the three of them were going on a school trip to a nearby ski resort. I prepared a large breakfast of pancakes and other goodies and called to them several times to come eat. Finally they came to the table looking very tired; they all said they weren't hungry. When I took them to the bus, they hardly said a word. Later that day, upon cleaning up where they had slept, I found several empty bottles of alcohol and cigarettes. It was as if an alarm went off within me. I could not believe my daughter would have even considered smoking or drinking. I thought for the next 24 hours on how I should approach her and address the seriousness of this kind of behavior.

I waited till Sunday evening when she was lying in bed to talk to her. Her father and I gently shared our feelings with her and said we would need to contact the other parents to let them know what had occurred. We explained the dangers of this type of behavior, as well as our intolerance of it. When we finished, she looked at us in total defiance and said, "I will smoke and drink whenever I want to." Once more that feeling that is unexplainable went through me. Where was my sweet and sensitive daughter who was playing with Barbie dolls just two years earlier?

This was the beginning of Lucy leaving us for a life without meaning and filled with self-destruction. For the remainder of that school year, I received periodic calls from the school principal reporting Lucy's disrespectful and defiant behavior, along with a noticeable lack of interest in her schoolwork. At the end of the school year, she had removed herself from other friendships and was only interested in spending time with her best friend, who had an older sister. She always wanted to spend time at their home where there were older girls and the parents were often out of the house. Her father and I felt a strong sense of unease with the situation, but at the same time our efforts were futile in changing it. By the end of that summer, Lucy had formed closer bonds with the older girls, and her best friend and her sister moved to Israel.

At the beginning of freshman year, all hell broke loose. Lucy was determined to spend time with the older girls instead of friends her age. On one occasion she went out with them and didn't return until the next day. We were up the entire night calling other parents in an effort to find her. One Sunday afternoon she went out for several hours, returning with glassy eyes and alcohol on her breath. After an intense confrontation, she took a variety of pills she found in the medicine cabinet and passed out. I thought she was dead; we rushed her to the hospital, where her stomach was pumped and the three of us spent the night.

This was the first of three admissions to the ER, a one-week stay in an adolescent psychiatric ward, two outpatient adolescent rehabs, and one ten-day inpatient rehab from her freshman to senior year of high school. Midway through her senior year we learned of her cocaine use. At this point her counselor informed us about an educational consultant who would come into the area, spend time with Lucy, and then advise us of an educational/rehabilitation program. His recommendation was to send Lucy to a program in Redlands, California. Our hearts sank; this was the hardest decision we had to make up to this point, but all our vigilant efforts to intervene and save Lucy from continuous self-destruction had been futile.

OUR EFFORTS AND THEIR IMPACT

WHEN LUCY WAS IN ninth grade, we decided to take her to our pediatrician, who had known Lucy from birth, for his advice. After informing him of our concerns, he consoled us and said, "Do not be too concerned; this behavior will pass." The following month we had Lucy evaluated by an adolescent psychiatrist at Western Psychiatric Institute and Clinic in Pittsburgh, but we received no advice or recommendation. At the beginning of tenth grade, I learned of another mother in the school district who was experiencing similar problems with her daughter and had placed her in a private school several hours away from Pittsburgh. I contacted the mother and from her learned of a highly recommended therapist in the area and also the name of the private school. Her father and I took her to see the school and also contacted the therapist. After the visit Lucy persuaded us not to send her to the school but was receptive to the counseling.

This decision led to three years of weekly therapy for Lucy, her father and me. On most occasions Lucy displayed more respect toward the therapist, Ann, than she did anyone else during this period of her life. This gave us an ounce of hope that all was not lost. Although it did not change Lucy's substance abuse, it was very beneficial in providing guidance to us in terms of setting boundaries and consequences. I later wished I had concentrated more on the benefit of consequences.

The therapist also referred us on to an adolescent psychiatrist who saw Lucy twice a month. The psychiatrist diagnosed her as having Attention Deficit Disorder and additionally ordered bimonthly drug testing. As her therapist, Ann, said early on, "We need to form a corral around Lucy, the corral being made up of therapist, psychiatrist, father, and mother in order to constantly make her aware of the boundaries. If she goes out of the boundary, there will be serious consequences." Later on the local magistrate also became a part of our corral. Fortunately, our community had a magistrate who had a very low tolerance for delinquent girls. Lucy from ninth through twelfth grade found herself on various occasions in the magistrate's office for such violations as smoking in the high-school restroom, smoking marijuana on a school field trip, and underage drinking. She had learned of the magistrate sending other girls from the high school to the Shuman Center located in a very scary section of Pittsburgh. It was described as a place where you were more or less "thrown to the wolves" and was one of the few possible consequences that seemed to affect Lucy's behavior for a while. After her last trip to the magistrate's office, there appeared to be a slight improvement lasting for several months.

The various rehabs she entered really seemed to have little effect. If anything, they merely provided us with respite from what Ann would often refer to as her "outrageous behavior."

During these high-school years, Lucy would drink alcohol or take any drug on the street that gave her an altered feeling, from marijuana to Ritalin, LSD, and cocaine. We never kept alcohol in the home with the exception of hiding wine in the rafters of the attic to have for special occasions, but she would always find it and proceed to drink the whole bottle.

An ongoing concern of ours was that Lucy would do so poorly in school that she would not be accepted to a college. As a result of my fear, I did many of her homework assignments, helped to write her papers, and did just about whatever it took to keep her from getting a failing grade. I often felt I was going through highschool all over again, only this time it was much more difficult. I never gave up the hope that in college she would find herself and everything would change. But that was never going to happen. In the beginning of her senior year, she was accepted into the Learning Disabled Program at Muskingham College based on her ADD. I remember that as being one of the happiest days of my life. I actually believed that once she left home and went to college that her behavior would change. By the end of her senior year, when she was in rehab in California, we knew she would be unable to enter school that fall, and it only got worse.

By the time Lucy was in eleventh grade, Ann recommended I seek counseling for myself. I actually believed my hypervigilant efforts to monitor and control Lucy's actions might change her behavior! I had become totally obsessed with my daughter's behavior to the point where I was depressed, unable to sleep, and would become enraged by my inability to change her life. As for my own existence, I was living in constant fear and panic over what was going to happen to my daughter. It was as if I was living in a bad dream from which I could not awake. One thought consumed me, I had to save her from herself.

Throughout these years I believed we could change Lucy's course. In fact, I was convinced we could. If only, if only, if only—how I exhausted my energies and financial resources trying to make the "if onlys" happen. I now realize there was nothing more we could have done as parents, nor was there anything more our society had to offer in addressing Lucy's problems that we had not already tried. Only Lucy could change her course. I now recognize that some of our children heed our advice and some must live the experience no matter how dreadful the consequence.

CALIFORNIA 1998

LUCY LEFT FOR BENCHMARK in Redlands, California, in February of her senior year. One month prior to this, I had received a phone call from Lucy's friend's mother, who was also having her daughter drug tested and in therapy. She informed me that Susan's most recent testing revealed the use of cocaine. Shortly after that call, I learned that they withdrew their daughter from the high school and placed her in an educational/psychiatric facility in an undisclosed, out-of-state location. The parents prevented any further contact between their daughter and her friends. Although this seemed like a drastic measure, I felt there would be a future benefit from this form of action.

Several weeks later, I opened the results of Lucy's bi-monthly drug testing. These also revealed the use of cocaine. Once more that unexplainable panic went through me. I immediately went to the high school, requested she be excused, and later that day informed them she would not be returning. Within a week, the three of us were on a plane to Los Angeles. We felt there was no other alternative. The days prior to leaving were emotionally and physically exhausting. I was determined to get Lucy there safely, never questioning my motivation. As for Lucy's father, I had never seen him more broken than the day we left her in California. He was inconsolable.

The school director was very strict and expected the parents as well as the students to abide by all rules. There was much we did not know about the program, and we went on blind faith that it just might turn Lucy's life around. After returning to Pittsburgh, we called the school director, who informed us they had placed Lucy in a rehab/detox setting. She would spend the next three months there, and we would not be allowed to talk to her for several weeks. Neither Lucy nor we had been informed of this prior to our leaving. We became even more sick-at-heart; we feared she would believe we had abandoned her. What had we done?

During the next three months, we corresponded by mail and eventually were allowed to talk by telephone once a week. Lucy seemed to have adjusted. My husband and I noticed a peace and quiet in our home, something we had not experienced in quite a few years, and eventually became more comfortable with our decision.

During this period of time, I enrolled Lucy in correspondence courses in order for her to obtain the number of credits necessary for her to graduate from the local high school in June. Against the rehabilitation school director's advice, we made the decision to allow her to come home and participate in her high school graduation. She promised to return with no problems after five days. She stayed true to her word, and the two of us flew back to California. Had I known how heartwrenching it would be for the two of us to part this time, I would have decided against this return trip home.

We arrived at the John Wayne Airport outside of Los Angeles the evening before Lucy was to return to school. For lack of very few rental cars from which to choose, we ended up with what most people would perceive as a pimp's car, somewhere between the size of the largest Cadillac and smallest limo! I could barely maneuver it out of the parking lot, much less drive it on an LA freeway. I reassured myself we would only have to go to the hotel, to Lucy's school, and back to the airport. We arose the next morning, and with much reluctance from Lucy and sadness within me, we drove back to the school. Upon entering the director's office, the director took one look at Lucy's face and said she was not allowed to return with a piercing. While Lucy was at home she had a ring put in her eyebrow; we did not say much about it, as it was very minor compared to everything she had done in the past. However, the director made it very clear the piercing had to be removed.

Lucy and I returned to the hotel, where we both tried to no avail to remove the ring. Our hands were shaking, and Lucy was crying and pleading with me not to take her back to the f—— school. Trying to remain calm, I searched in the Yellow Pages under tattoo parlors. After several calls I was successful in finding a man who said he would remove the ring. He gave me directions to a parlor located somewhere in the foothills off the freeway. This is the only experience that is even remotely funny when I reflect on the past. Here I was in this huge car (which felt like the width of one lane), on a ten-lane expressway, in what seemed like a foreign country, looking for a tattoo parlor. To add to my anxiety, Lucy was getting more anxious and irritated by the minute. When we finally arrived at this seedy-looking parlor, a young man, who looked like my childhood vision of the devil, opened the door. He was dressed in all black with a red pitchfork painted on his T-shirt, long dyed-black hair, and rings and tattoos on every visible part of his body. After a half hour in a back room, Lucy returned with the ring removed. As we drove back to the school, she once more started crying and pleading with me not to take her back. I tried in every way to console her, but with each minute I was becoming more upset at the thought of leaving her.

When we entered the lobby of the school, everyone was staring at us; we were both crying and inconsolable. How could I leave her there? That night all I could do was pray to God that I would wake up the next morning feeling I had done the right thing.

Many decisions that parents make at different times in their child's life are difficult and plagued with uncertainty, but the decisions we must make as parents of a young adult struggling with drug addiction are, in addition, accompanied by much pain and anguish.

Lucy remained in the program four more months. It was a Saturday afternoon in September when we received a call from the school director. Lucy had run away and was believed to be staying at a motel with another student who had left several weeks earlier. Because of her leaving without permission, she would not be allowed to return. In total dismay we thought, *Where is she? Will she call? And where do we go from here?* The next day we received a call from Lucy asking that she be allowed to come home. We did not want to reward her for this outrageous behavior but knew we had no alternative other than to let her return. We contacted the local bus station in California, wired them money for a ticket, and arranged for her return. We hoped that a four-day bus trip across the United States would give her ample opportunity to reflect on her actions.

When Lucy returned she reconnected with some friends and took a job at a local coffee shop. All seemed well. After several weeks we decided to take the girls to Cape May, New Jersey, for a short family vacation. While away, Lucy decided to stop taking her Ritalin due to her inability to take the medication as pre-scribed. She admitted that a prescription that should have lasted a month was gone in a week. Had she made some progress? Her father and I were both encouraged by this unexpected and healthy decision. It was also during this week that her father noticed a protrusion on the upper portion of his chest. With each day it became more painful and debilitating. Several weeks later he was diagnosed with Stage 4 lung cancer that had advanced to the lymph nodes and bone areas.

Over the course of the next eight months, my focus on Lucy diminished. Our family bonded closely, and my husband's comfort and quality of life became my priority. Lucy continued to work and decided to move into an apartment with several of her friends. She would come to spend time with us regularly, was always available when needed, and did everything she could to make her father more comfortable. My sister, who I have always believed to be one of the greatest gifts in my life, called one day and said that she and my brother-in-law wanted to give us two first class airline tickets to wherever we wished to travel. We made arrangements to go to Florida for the month of February and the girls came and stayed with us for a week. The four of us were so blessed to be able to spend this most valuable time together. By spring the cancer was rapidly progressing. Lucy's father died in June.

Both girls moved back to the house, where the three of us lived together for the next six months. Lisa became engaged to be married, and Lucy, upon my advice, decided to go to a massage therapy school in Virginia Beach. During the six months she was living at home and working, I encouraged her to pursue a career where she would use her hands. Always having mystical tendencies in my thinking, I felt this particular massage training program could have a positive influence on Lucy due to its holistic and spiritual approach. During the next eight months of school, she completed and passed all requirements, made new friends, graduated in August, and returned home just in time for her sister's September wedding.

THE SPIRAL DOWNWARD

UP TO THIS POINT I had chosen to think of Lucy's drug abuse as "bad behavior." When I thought of addiction, I would think of individuals in prison, sleeping on a park bench, or dying from an overdose. I knew that Lucy smoked marijuana, probably on a daily basis, and I would talk to her on every open occasion about the habit and the repercussions; but she saw no harm in her behavior and compared it to one having a glass of wine or bottle of beer. Most of the time I tried to bury my concerns, slowly realizing I wasn't going to change anything.

Upon her return to Pittsburgh after graduating from the massage therapy program, Lucy spent much of her time with a girl she had met while previously working at the coffee shop. Most of her high school friends were either away at school or married. A year later, I learned, through the association with this friend, she had access to just about any illegal or prescription drug available. She and her friend became inseparable. The man with whom her friend was living had an Oxycontin addiction, which was conveniently being supported by his friend, who was a physician. The friend and boyfriend would pay Lucy with drugs to babysit their four-year-old. Throughout the next year Lucy continued to live at home with noticeable changes occurring in her behavior. On many occasions she would display frustration, impatience, and aggression for no explainable reason.

That winter Lisa, Lucy, and I took a trip to Sedona and the Grand Canyon. During this trip, Lucy would sometimes refuse to go out with us, and for lack of any other description she was impossible to get along with. At home, she was unable to stick with any effort toward improving her life, from taking courses at the local community college to several attempts at working. She would become emotionally upset and sometimes run to the bathroom and throw up. I was at a loss to understand this behavior, thinking it could be depression, and encouraged her to see a psychiatrist. She went on an antidepressant but showed no improvement.

Lucy also had several car accidents during this time, once totaling a new SUV I had purchased on her twenty-first birthday. She was taken by ambulance to the hospital for observation. While with her in the ER, she became very belligerent toward me because they were going to release her without a prescription for pain. She had no visible pain. Several weeks later her friend came to our house claiming Lucy had stolen money from her purse. When I confronted her with the friend's accusation she confessed that she had been taking "these pills" for some time from which she could not withdraw. She stayed on the sofa for several days complaining of having the flu. This was the beginning of addiction as I had never witnessed.

Over the next five months both of our lives were out of control. Lucy was stealing my money, checks, and other items of value that she could pawn. She would leave the house after a confrontation and not return for several days. She would often become aggressive and verbally abusive. I felt traumatized and was unable to share the extent of her behavior with anyone. Instead I would call the city police and tell them my daughter was going to the North side to buy drugs and could they not do something? I contacted local mental health clinics and hospitals to learn of any help. I could not believe they were unable to offer any program suggestions or advice. I decided to contact Lucy's therapist, Ann, from years past, who advised me to get her into a rehab facility as soon as possible. I finally persuaded Lucy to go to a local facility about twenty miles from our home. We sat there for the better part of the day waiting for our insurance company's approval. All the time I was praying she would not get up and run. At five o'clock they admitted her, and I went home exhausted. At midnight the phone rang. It was the night counselor calling to tell me I needed to pick Lucy up immediately as they had found pills in her possession.

In reflection, what I should have done during this period of time and would do now, without a second thought, would be to have her arrested. Jail is a serious consequence for seriously bad behavior. I have learned now it can sometimes be one of the most effective consequences.

I felt sheer desperation, not knowing what to do or where to turn. I was unable to discuss the seriousness of my situation with close family or friends. How *could they or anyone possibly understand what was happening?* I felt so alone, no longer having the compassion and support of Lucy's father. Only he, as her parent, could possibly understand what I was feeling, and he was gone. There were days I felt emotionally paralyzed. I was going through the motions of getting up and going to work but my functioning was well below a normal level. My fears were no longer just for my daughter but also for myself. I became convinced one of us was not going to survive the repercussions of her addictive behavior. I once more consulted Ann. Her advice was to investigate long-term rehab facilities at a further distance from Pittsburgh. I eventually told Lucy she could no longer live at our house and her only alternative would be rehabilitation. She had no income and nowhere to live. I allowed her to do her own research on different facilities. She chose a six-month program in California. Within several days I drove her to the airport, praying every minute she would get on the plane. This time there were no tears. We both desperately needed separation and recovery.

Lucy remained in the program for six months. After the first month she and another patient ran away and were later picked up, by one of the program counselors, hitchhiking along the freeway to LA. After that she was transferred to one of their more remote locations. She had developed a close relationship with a young man from New Jersey who was also there for rehab. He had been there for nine months and was thought to be doing quite well. One night he left the facility, drove into LA, overdosed on heroin, and died. Lucy was devastated.

Upon Lucy's graduation from the program, I presented her with two choices: remain in California, where she would stay closely connected with the program and work; or move to Cleveland and live with her sister until she could find a job and get a place of her own. She chose to move to Cleveland. With the exception of some anxiety and periodic panic attacks, she remained well and was self-supportive for about fifteen months.

One weekend when visiting Lucy, however, I noticed the same behavior I had in the past: somewhat withdrawn, agitated, and argumentative. By the end of the weekend, she broke down and confessed to her renewed use of opiates and the inability to stop. It was back to another rehab facility in Ohio, where after one month she left against their advice. Within the next three months she lost her job and became nonfunctional.

I had read an article earlier in the year that mentioned a physician in Cleveland who was treating heroin addicts with a new drug called Suboxone. It was used to ease the addict off the drug through minimizing the withdrawal. I contacted his office and was advised to have Lucy admitted to a nearby psychiatric hospital, where he would do an evaluation. It took almost a week to get the insurance company's approval and for a bed to become available. During this period of time, Lucy became violently ill from the withdrawal. Having no alternative, I actually gave her money to buy the drugs she needed while waiting to be admitted. I could not risk losing this opportunity of a treatment that just might work. After several weeks Lucy was released and referred to a psychiatrist who would see her twice a month for continuation on the Suboxone.

When Suboxone first became FDA approved, a physician had to receive a certification in order to prescribe this treatment, and there were very few physicians in any given locality who had this certification. To this day, I believe Suboxone has helped many people gradually overcome their addiction. These are the individuals who have a strong desire to recover and stay well. However, many therapists will argue it is still a form of addiction and makes a person drug dependent. It is also often abused by addicts who use it intermittently in order to get high whenever they want.

Over the next four years I believe I went into a period of complete denial. I still did not understand the many sides of addiction nor did I have the desire or courage to learn. I am also certain I went into this denial based on the fears of reliving the trauma of the past. I felt I had lost my energy to fight this battle. I shifted my thinking from Lucy struggling with addiction to Lucy just having "emotional problems." It was a safer and more protective approach for both of us.

For two of these years, Lucy lived alone in Ohio, returning to Pittsburgh in the fall of 2005. I sold the small condo I had purchased for her in Cleveland and bought a townhouse where she could live and be close to our family. This only proved to be another futile attempt to help my daughter. The " if onlys" were once more taking over my thoughts in my effort to understand her existence. If only she would get a job, if only she would go to school, if only she would fall in love. The " if onlys" would be a cure for my "troubled" daughter. I just didn't get it! I could not grasp or accept the "if onlys" were never going to happen nor did I have the power to make them happen. Neither of us was open to the reality of her situation, Lucy of her drug usage, to escape herself and the world in which she lived, and I in my denial of it. For days and weeks at a time I would become so tormented and depressed over her chronic state of dysfunction.

I now realize most of my efforts toward what I thought would help Lucy were enabling her to stay addicted. My continual assistance and financial support in every area of her life may have eased my anxieties, but it was also detrimental to both of us. I was trying so hard to add normality to the life of a totally dysfunctional human being. I could not bear the thought that this would be the form of her of existence for the rest of her life.

Lucy would isolate herself, not answering our attempts to reach her, for days at a time. I would try to convince her to go to school if for no other reason than to just be around other people. Sometimes she agreed and would enroll in classes, but after several months she would quit, blaming it on some physical ailment. She never went out socially with the exception of family gatherings, which was often accompanied by much coaxing. I was convinced she was severely depressed and found a physician in Pittsburgh who continued her treatment with the Suboxone while also treating her for the ADD and depression. After she made several visits to his office, he diagnosed Lucy as bipolar. He tried her on several different medications, causing her to gain fifty pounds and become borderline diabetic, with no visible change in her behavior. Sometime during this period she decided to stop taking the Suboxone. She continued smoking marijuana while taking Adderall for the ADD, Klonopin for the anxiety and panic attacks, and Seroquel for what was believed to be a bipolar condition.

I now believe the disease of addiction is often mistaken for bipolar disorder. Addicts are never honest about the true nature of their problems, and the highs and lows they complain of mimic bipolar disorder. Also addiction and bipolar disorder are generally first noticed and diagnosed in young adulthood.

After one and a half years of treating Lucy for bipolar disorder with no success, her physician referred her on to a psychiatrist at the local mental health clinic. While he didn't reveal his suspicions, I think he may have suspected her emotional problems were a result of addiction. I later learned she had made application over the Internet for her own credit cards. This was at a time in our nation's history when almost anyone, including those claiming they were students with or without income, could obtain credit. This enabled her to order medications online from Canada with no one's knowledge.

For a period of seven months, Lucy was ordering Ultram and Flexeril in quantities of one hundred on a regular basis. Simultaneously she continued taking Adderall, Klonopin, and Cymbalta prescribed by the psychiatrist. On various occasions she would call and complain of having cuts, bruises, or a swollen tongue for no apparent reason. Or she would find herself on the floor without memory of falling. At first I thought this was all an exaggeration, but later became concerned and told her to discuss this with her physician, though she never did. Somehow Lucy survived what could have caused her death.

In January of 2008, Lucy came to pick me up at the airport. When I got in the car, she began to describe an unusual feeling she had experienced that morning that she felt was starting to occur once more. She was driving in the middle lane of a three-lane expressway, and as I looked over at Lucy, her legs and arms contracted toward her body and her eyes rolled back into her head. My first thought was a stroke or heart attack. I somehow took control of the car long enough to exit the highway and call 911. When the ambulance arrived Lucy was slowly regaining consciousness, having no idea what had just occurred. We spent that night in the hospital where she had two more grand mal seizures. The tests performed over the next several days indicated she had had previous seizures, and she was diagnosed with a seizure disorder. There was no drug testing done; if there had been, it would have revealed an excessive amount of drugs in her system. Instead she was given an antiseizure medication and released. Her driving privileges were also revoked for six months, during which time she would be seen by a neurologist.

Over the course of the next month, Lucy spent more time with me, and I began to notice the same type of antagonistic and aggressive behavior I had noticed years earlier. As much as I did not want to believe she was using illegal drugs, I felt the need to know the truth behind her behavior and recent complaints. I did a search of her purse while she was asleep and found the bottles of Ultram and Flexeril. Both had been mailed to her earlier the same week and were empty. I also discovered she had taken a one-month's supply of Adderall in less than a week.

At this point I knew Lucy's drug abuse was out of control and had caused the seizures. When I tried to confront her, I immediately realized her denial and defenses would make her unapproachable for any form of logical discussion. I knew I had to find a place she would be safe while I could work out a plan to get her into a rehab facility. I took her to her sister's in Cleveland. Within several days she began to display psychotic behavior producing hallucinations. Lisa and I both did our own research on the side effects of the known medications Lucy had been taking. We learned that Adderall, taken in large quantities, could produce hallucinations. Also an overdose of Ultram could produce seizures and had the potential to "cause psychic and physical dependence of the morphine type." Further:

> The drug has been associated with craving drug-seeking behavior and tolerance development and should be not be used in opioid dependent patients. Ultram can reinstate physical dependence in patients that have been previously dependent or chronically using opioids. Physicians' Desk Reference 2008 Medical Economics Company

To the best of my knowledge, what Lucy had been doing at least a year prior to the seizure occurrence was using heroin when she had the access to buy it; she would then substitute the Ultram and other drugs to combat the withdrawal when the heroin was gone.

Once Lucy was in Cleveland, I contacted a local support group I had read about in our newspaper called SOS, Sunlight of the Spirit. I often believe it was divine intervention that led me to my first meeting. From the moment I joined the five other mothers who were in the group that morning, I experienced comfort and support. Opening up to what I had lived through for longer than I could believe was a life-changing experience. At last I found hope for myself.

During the week Lucy stayed at Lisa's, we did what can best be described as a family intervention, the three of us—me, my daughter, and my son-in-law—protecting Lucy from herself. Lisa threw away all the drugs she could find with the exception of the antiseizure medication and never left Lucy alone. Simultaneously I contacted the mental health clinic where Lucy had been seen and called the local authorities to see what options we had in the event Lucy would not cooperate with rehabilitation. After collecting the facts I needed, I created an outline for Lucy to review. I had to break through her denial, which is nearly impossible when dealing with addiction. The outline presented her current addiction, including records of her online drug purchases, results of her addiction, actions taken by us in defense of ourselves, and three options from which she could choose upon returning to Pittsburgh. I was going on the hope that when presented with the undeniable facts of her behavior, Lucy would realize her need for help and choose rehab.

She made the best choice. I drove her home from Cleveland, and two days later she and I left for Wernersville, Pennsylvania, to a facility called Caron. I had first contacted Hazelden in Minnesota, and their admission counselor advised me of Caron, a facility that was modeled after Hazelden and located in Pennsylvania. Several years earlier I had seen Christopher Kennedy Lawford interviewed on the Larry King show. He spoke about a book he had just written called *Symptoms of Withdrawal* and praised a rehab facility where he had turned for help. I remembered quickly writing down the name of the treatment center and had it tucked away in my desk drawer; it was Caron.

RECOVERY

GETTING MOST ADDICTS TO a rehab facility is never an easy task and Lucy was no exception. The morning she left, the drama started. She fought me from the moment she awoke, only this time we had a five-hour trip in the car together. All I could do was inhale deep breaths, stay very firm and collected, and pray that we would make it without any undesirable event. I have no idea what she took that morning, but once we were on our way she became drowsy and barely spoke until our arrival.

From the moment I walked through the door into Caron I knew I had brought Lucy to the right place.

This was the beginning of not only Lucy's recovery but also mine. They describe the program as being "the first of many doors you and your family will walk through on your path of recovery." This was the first of Lucy's rehabs that engaged the family in the patient's recovery. They offered a five-day family education program where together we learned about the disease of addiction and its effects on the family, the impact of codependency, the relapse process, and prevention and recovery. Through the education and family therapy, I was able to grasp the impact this disease has not only on the addict but also on the family. For five days Lucy, Lisa, and I sat in a circle with seven other families sharing our experiences. Up to this point I had been "living in the closet" when it came to Lucy's behavior. I came to realize that so much of my behavior, in an effort to add happiness to her existence, had only perpetuated her problems. It was also the first opportunity for Lisa to speak out about the impact addiction had on her life. I realized how blind I must have become to any problems my older daughter may have been experiencing. Together Lisa and I learned what we had to do to help and protect ourselves.

Lucy remained at Caron for five weeks and was then transferred to one of their long-term rehab programs, Renaissance, in Boca Raton, Florida. During the course of Lucy's treatment, Lisa and I attended family week, where we were again involved in a three-day intensive program. This program was designed to reinforce healthy interactions and effective ways of supporting recovery rather than enabling addiction. Also part of the treatment included weekly calls to Lisa and me from Lucy's therapist, continually reinforcing what we needed to do as family members to promote Lucy's wellness.

Lucy remained at Renaissance for five months. Once her therapist felt she was ready, she was required to go out and find a job enabling her to become self-supportive. She found a job within several weeks, left the program, and found a halfway house for women. This was her first opportunity in years to experience a sense of self-worth and capability. She continued seeing her therapist on a regular basis and had two relapses within the next year, the first leading to detox and further treatment, the second resulting in her going back on the Suboxone. That was two years prior to the time of this writing. During those two years she remained in Florida and went back to school in order to become licensed as a massage therapist. In the summer of 2010, she took the National Boards and became licensed in the state of Florida where she worked for the next year.

CONCLUSIONS

ONLY ANOTHER PARENT OF a young adult struggling with addiction can understand the p....... d emotional pain, frustration, and confusion we experience while watching our children destroy their lives. My obsession with Lucy's problem over the years became my addiction, one moment feeling intense pity and sadness the next anger and frustration. During Lucy's first week at Caron, her therapist called me and asked that I write a letter to Lucy describing how her addiction had impacted my life. After giving this much thought I wrote the following:

For many years I have felt like I was living two lives, yours and mine. This has been mentally and physically exhausting, and I have been at a loss as to how to change this pattern. I absorb your emotions, pay for all your expenses, try to solve your problems, and worse than anything else live with the profound sadness of the impact addiction has had on your life. There is no area of your life that has not been impacted, but I believe those that take priority are as follows:

- *Lack of meaningful relationships with others. Drugs have become your substitute for friends, but they will never make up for the resulting loneliness.*
- *Loss of trust from those you love.*
- *Lack of career. Your failure in all attempts to build a career, despite your strong denial of this fact, has been a result of continual substance abuse. I believe the feeling of failure is always pulling you down. Please open yourself to the reasons.*

- *Lack of sense of purpose or accomplishment. Substance abuse has been your escape from all unpleasant feelings we must experience in order to grow. What you have been unable to realize is it continues to take you down to a lower level of functioning and understanding. Addiction has robbed you of the ability to gain courage and build strength over your fears and insecurities. Instead of building coping skills throughout the past fourteen years, you have relied exclusively on chemicals.*
- *I will love and support you throughout every step of your recovery but will never turn back to behavior patterns that may have kept you safe but also kept you addicted.*

Lisa was also asked to describe the impact Lucy's addiction had on her, and she wrote this:

Over the past fourteen years I've lived with being the "good sister" and the responsibility that comes along with that label I never asked for. I've dealt with the terrible worry for your well-being…fearing that one of these days you won't wake up or that I'll get a call you're in jail or have been raped or attacked by one of your "associates." I have watched your illness impact Mommy and Daddy in irreversible ways. I feel at such a loss…We're sisters, but I know I have become detached over the years—my way of protecting myself, I suppose. But due to your drug abuse you have remained stuck in life, and instead of growing our relationship through shared experiences like family, friends, career, etc., we ultimately have very little in common. Your drug abuse has impacted every area of your life, and your denial of this fact is truly frustrating…

What could our family have done differently to prevent Lucy's illness? I do not know. Prevention of this growing problem is so important, but the reality is, not one of us knows what we could have done to prevent our child's addiction. However, what I have come to believe is how we react, once we suspect addictive behavior, can be of vital importance. Opening ourselves up to receive education on addiction and seeking support from the professional community and others going through the same experience is the best advice one parent can give to another.

My conclusions based on my experiences are these:

- Education about addiction should be incorporated into every school's curriculum beginning at the elementary level.
- Rehab programs offer vital education and are the first step toward recovery regardless of age.
- There will be relapses in the majority of addicts.
- With each relapse will come a consequence.
- Always allow the addict to suffer the consequences regardless of the discomfort and pain it may cause for us as parents.
- Because of the consequences the addict will give more thought before using the next time, and periods of recovery will become longer.
- We must come to the realization that our efforts can be futile until the addict has the desire for change.

- Once we as parents make the changes to help ourselves, we open a door for changes within our child.

Lucy, 32, returned to the Pittsburgh area in 2011 where she has been gainfully employed and totally self-supportive for almost two years. One of the greatest contributing factors in her recovery was her living at a distance for three years. Through addressing her addiction to drugs, over an extended period of time, she was able to become independent. This provided her with the opportunity to set goals for herself, attain these goals, and experience the success from her effort.

I am very grateful for our current relationship and place a high value on the time we spend together. We have both learned to be respectful of one another's boundaries, which helps us through times of conflict. Sometimes I need to remind myself of what Chris, our therapist, once said to me. "You cannot control Lucy's destiny." In summary, I do not look into the past very often, embrace the meaning of "living each day to its fullest," and place Lucy's and my future in the hands of God.

Karen

Hope is some extraordinary grace
that God gives us to control our
fears, not oust them.
Vincent McNabb

PATRICK

CHILDHOOD AND
BACKGROUND INFORMATION

IN THE BEGINNING I felt like hope was almost
dead—*not* hope never lost. I felt like my situation with
my son and my husband was unique and no one really
understood. I remember being at an NA meeting in
those early days and beginning to tell my "unique"
story when pretty much everyone else in the room
began nodding and smiling and under their breath
muttering, "Been there, done that." It sort of pissed
me off. I clammed up after that and diverted to my
husband (my third husband, which, of course, I felt
added to my unique situation). I had been dragging
him to these meetings so I assumed he wouldn't add

anything too substantial when to my surprise he said something profound:

"I always thought these kids were doing drugs because all they wanted to do was have fun getting high. Here I was working myself to death and my twenty-six-year-old stepson was getting high. I now realize these kids are getting high to stop the pain, to get some relief, and that they don't want to live like they are—they can't seem to get off the spiral." *Wow*, I thought, *he really does understand*.

I understood, in my heart, my son's reasons for getting high. I thought he was different, maybe "better" than all those other drug addicts. My son was/is generous, loving, smart, caring, mannerly, curious, gullible, a little naïve, sweet, and has a very, very good heart. I felt, and still feel, that he is a fourteen year old in a thirty-year-old body.

Patrick also has attention deficit disorder. He suffers from anxiety, low self-esteem, and depression. *HELLO...* I felt so sorry for him that as my son was growing, I helped, inadvertently, to mold him into the inadequate and totally unprepared adult he had become. I had tons of hope for myself in helping him; I just didn't understand that I was contributing to my son's feeling of hopelessness on his own.

I think of myself as being capable, intelligent, and a doer. So I took these to the extreme and used my "qualities" to "protect" my son's feeling of inadequacy and failure. I should be honest and admit that a bit of that was to assuage my guilt over providing my son with the life that I thought helped to screw him up.

I didn't realize that my situation was no more or less unique than anyone else's. My son's father and I divorced when Patrick was four. The divorce resulted from affairs Patrick's father had and my discovery of an eighteen-month-old baby by a "friend" of the family. As everyone knows, when parents divorce, the guilt begins to set in and the kids reap the rewards.

I remarried a couple years later to the man I thought was my knight in shining armor. In that time, Patrick had to deal with divorce, my ex's new family (too much to mention here), Patrick's own confusion and eventual diagnosis of ADD, med trials, a new school, and my new husband. I was married to husband number two for ten years—the most formative years of my son's life. Damn...another guilt-producing fact. During this period, both my son and I learned about excess, irresponsibility, and unaccountability, lost fear of authority, and me, me, me.

I thought husband number two was sent from heaven to make up for the first husband to whom I was married. We traveled; bought every new technology; replaced things just because we wanted new ones; enjoyed a pool, horses, a big house, and lots of fancy cars; sent my son to private schools; confronted teachers when I felt he was mistreated, etc., etc., etc.

It turned out that this marriage had all the perks because husband number two was as much of a playboy as husband number one, only he could hide it better and could give us things to basically make up for his "faults." Patrick was a young teenager by this time and was learning lots of things: *men cheat, women take it for as long as they can, money means everything, you need to always look good, pretend everything is A-OK, and stuff your feelings inside*, among a million other bad habits.

During all this time, Patrick was the light of my life. I was so proud of him. All the teachers loved him and sent notes home praising his actions, manners, and diligence. He had so many interests: collecting valuable basketball cards, playing basketball, identifying bugs and insects, fishing, writing stories, reading. He loved reptiles and was top ranked in video games. He was very trusting and would do pretty much whatever was asked.

We did so much together and so thoroughly enjoyed each other's company that we slowly but surely became enmeshed. Our circles were so crossed that there was little room for our individual lives to flourish. When divorce number two happened, I thought of my son as much more mature than his actual years and confided things that I should not have as an adult and as a parent. He was my sounding board, my unconditional best friend—more guilt-producing ammunition.

Patrick was a freshman in high school when I met my third husband. My son had not yet used drugs, smoked cigarettes, or used alcohol. He was still the sweet kid as always but was showing signs of sadness, disappointment, and feeling like he was different. He said he'd always felt different, but in high school it really began to show. He thought when kids got older they would act more mature and stop being so mean and thoughtless. He couldn't wait to "grow up" because he thought when you become an adult, all of a sudden everything would fall into place and people would do and say the right things and be nice to each other. This was not the case in high school. I can still remember, as if it were yesterday, my fifteen-, sixteen-, seventeen-year-old son, who was six feet five inches, crying over someone being mean.

My contribution to my son's needing to deaden his pain was trying too hard to make up for his growing sadness. He had been to therapy ever since he was five years old. In high school his therapist said he had low-grade dysthymia (a continual sadness or low-grade depression). He was on Adderall for ADD and an antidepressant. He was more and more anxious and began to show signs of anger.

Husband number three and I married a year later when my son was a junior in high school. My son didn't have much of a relationship with his dad, who lived in a neighboring state. My new husband is wonderful (thank God) and began to fill in the father role. Soon, there were two men in my life who both wanted the number-one spot. In the early years of our marriage, it was hard but loving. I was beginning to do the things that I should have been doing all those years earlier. I was not focusing all my attention on my son. My husband showed me that I was smothering my son, babying him too much, in some ways even emasculating him. I was a mother bringing up a son who needed a father badly.

Beginning of Addictive Behavior

PATRICK WAS CONFLICTED INSIDE. He loved my husband (a very good role model, loving but firm, with very obvious values and boundaries) but fell back into old patterns of getting his own way and unaccountability. And a new vice popped up: showing anger. He moved in with his dad when he felt we were too "strict" and began to hold him accountable. We let him go, with love. In six months he was back, after an altercation with his drunken dad. When he came back, his sadness was more present than ever. My sadness for him grew right along with his.

When Patrick moved back home, he had some problems with underage drinking. He hung around with a crowd we were familiar with and thought the kids had good parents. We also knew that everyone experimented with alcohol at some point, and we didn't take this too seriously. Now I know better. Many kids that experiment with drugs or alcohol do just that—experiment. But when you combine drugs and/or alcohol with other medications, mood disorders, anxiety, depression, low self-esteem, and any other number of mental states, it is more likely the experiment will turn out to be an addiction.

Even though I felt my son was not ready for college, I caved in and allowed him to go. Enabling at its best! We sent him to a university in Florida that had a highly rated ADD support program.

Patrick didn't make it after the first semester. He was asked to leave because of "theft." He and another kid—high from the night before—borrowed a friend's car without permission, and the owner reported it missing. When the girl realized who had borrowed the car, she wanted to drop the charges but her parents pursued it. This is a good example of the kind of trouble my son would get into. He was a bystander, a go-along-with-the-group kind of kid, in the wrong place at the wrong time. I fell for all of these excuses, and they only seemed to confirm my deepest fear: Patrick could not take care of himself.

We tried to set limits. When Patrick was home, he would have to be in the house by a certain time at night or stay out. We thought he'd come home—and were surprised to find him asleep in the car or on the front steps or on the lounge in the backyard. He became hard to manage; we couldn't count on what he said or count on him to do what he needed to do.

My husband became exasperated. I was too, but I continued my job of protecting my son's feelings. We acted as if talking to him and having him understand what he was doing would change his behavior. I knew he *wanted* to change.

My husband guessed Patrick was coming home high. I thought, *No way. If he were high he wouldn't come into our room to say he was home and good night*. My husband guessed Patrick's inability to do anything productive was because he was high. I thought, *No way. He has ADD and is just confused*. My husband said my son was not grateful for all that we had been doing, and I thought, *No way. He is just used to getting everything he wants.*

We could no longer live under the same roof. Patrick was twenty-one; he moved back to where his dad lived and got an apartment. I visited him often and each time could see a slow decline in his life. His place was a mess. Furniture that had been given to him was broken. His car had unrepaired fender benders and ashtrays overflowing with cigarette butts. His clothes smelled, and he was oblivious to it all. He forgot to check his mail, and his phone would be turned off. There was always a crisis that really wasn't his fault. He used his ADD as his excuse of choice, and so did I.

While he was living there, he was put on an anti-anxiety medication. That was the beginning of the end. He *loved* this medication. Now he was taking Adderall during the day and Klonopin in the evening to settle him down. Since we lived in another state, we didn't know all this while it was happening. I was fully focused on the fact that Patrick was falling apart on his own and needed someone (me) to help him survive.

One Thanksgiving Day, I drove out to have dinner with him. While driving he called me from jail to say he had been arrested. He had been injecting heroin for over a year and was finally caught. UNBELIEVABLE.

BEGINNING OF REHAB

PATRICK'S FATHER BAILED HIM out of jail, and he stayed with my husband and I while attending a local outpatient rehab center. The program lasted six weeks, and during that time my son mostly lounged on the sofa watching TV, explaining that he was "dope sick." Needless to say, I have many of my son's gullible and naïve qualities. Later, he admitted to taking "pills" offered him at the rehab center by other patients while loitering in the parking lot, and the sofa time was his "crash" time.

After he completed the outpatient treatment, Patrick moved back to his apartment and lived there for a couple more years. Since he wasn't under our nose, we couldn't see what was going on, but the same red flags were there: messy house, smelly clothes, and one job after another. His dad bought him a car, and he totaled it (legally it wasn't his fault, but I don't think his responses were as sharp as they should have been).

Finally, Patrick said he had had enough and wanted to move back in with us, go to college, and start his adult life on the right track. He said all the things we wanted to hear. He sounded genuine, and I think he was. All his friends were moving on, and he was still stuck. He moved back with us without a car, cell phone, or any perks that he did not earn.

He was like a different kid, and we couldn't believe it. My husband and I thought he had learned his lessons and was on the road to adulthood. He quit smoking and became engrossed in working out and having a healthy body. He washed all his clothes—every single item—to get rid of the smell. After a few months we asked him if he'd like to take a community college course. He agreed, became engrossed in learning, and got an A. He was home or with us most of the time and did not contact any friends or have any outside influence. He applied to a private, small, local college and was accepted. He took two classes. Once again, he became engrossed and did very well. We got him a cell phone. I was driving him to school and back. After the first year of college and doing so well, we began looking for an apartment for him near campus and leased him a car. We were so thrilled with his success.

Patrick wanted an apartment away from school so that he had privacy and kids couldn't just walk over and distract him, but we also thought he should have a place within walking distance of school so that if something happened with the car (we were still cautious) he could walk to class. We bought a small house for him to live in a couple blocks off campus. Now, he had a fully furnished new house, a new car, cell phone, and freedom.

During the first semester at the new house, his grades slipped, but not by much. He asked if he could move back to our house for the summer even though his house was only twenty minutes away. We told him that he needed to work out his life on his own; we would help with advice, etc., but he couldn't keep running whenever he had the urge. He never explained why he wanted to move back home; he just wanted a break.

In hindsight this is what was going on: he couldn't keep up with taking care of a house, yard work, a full load of classes (he didn't want to take a full semester because he felt it might be too much, but we insisted), and managing new friends who bombarded him continually because he had a house. My son was twenty-five years old, and all the other kids were normal college age.

Also, the next-door neighbor sold drugs from their garage. My son never told us any of this. We just knew he wanted to "run" again, and we said no. During

Patrick's second semester, he crashed. He passed two classes but didn't complete the other two. We could see he was in distress and allowed him to move back home. He asked to take a break from school for a semester. We agreed, and he got a job at the local gym. When fall came around, he said he did not think he could handle school right now and did not want to go back or live in the house anymore.

He was using again but trying to keep it together. He was adamant about not using heroin, but of course, he was. Things went missing from our house with no explanation. Patrick became quiet, secretive, and lethargic. Finally, he said he needed to go back to rehab. In the next two years he was in and out of the local rehab, halfway houses, crashing with friends, back to rehab, the halfway house, and so on. Patrick was a challenge in rehab. He flirted with girls against the rules, passed notes, went out to smoke when he wasn't supposed to, and because of his extensive therapy, became what he thought was a rehab guru.

I was a total mess. I felt like my son was one step away from dying. I thought the next call I received would be the police telling me he was in the hospital, overdosed, dead, or in jail. I learned in NA and in my codependent group that this worry is common. My husband and I changed the locks on our doors.

I remember reading a recovery book in which a mother said she had to come to terms with the fact that her son was not the same sweet, innocent little kid she remembered, but someone completely different. I was beginning to have the same feelings. I wanted to let Patrick go, but the worry of him physically or even mentally harmed was more than I could handle.

We learned that Patrick did overdose in a car with some other kids from his halfway house and they dumped him behind an abandoned building in the middle of the night. Thank God they had the sense to call the police to tell them there was someone passed out in the alley.

Finally, we gave Patrick an ultimatum: go to Hazelden or we would distance ourselves from him and withhold any future support. He agreed and left the next day.

While he was at Hazelden, I found my saving grace: a codependent women's group that met once a week. There were other mothers in this group with kids just like mine. I felt immediately at home. Even though I had been going to some NA and Al-Anon meetings and confided in friends, I was not getting the relief I so desperately needed.

Along with attending this group, I also attended private sessions when I needed them (when I was going out of my mind). I read every book I could on codependency and understanding addicts.

Patrick got kicked out of Hazelden after only one month. He was not cooperative, didn't want to do chores or get up early, and wouldn't stop talking to the girls. When they called me and told me he was sitting in the office with his bags packed, I said a silent prayer to myself and told them to tell my son to have fun in Minnesota. To my surprise, I was fine when I got off the phone. I found myself becoming angrier than I was sad or feeling sorry for him.

MY TRANSFORMATION

HOPE WAS ALIVE AND kicking for the first time in ages!

Hazelden sent Patrick to a behavioral rehab in Mississippi. We agreed to pay for this rehab after Patrick agreed to stay there at least a month. He did, and flew home (where he got the money I don't know) on the thirty-first day. When he called to tell me this news, I told him he could not live with us, nor were we helping him in anyway—and that I loved him. He said he had it all taken care of; he was going back to the local rehab and would go where they recommended. I said fine and I love you.

Patrick called at three a.m. the next morning to tell me he was stuck at the airport and needed a ride. It felt like the same old damn crap was happening all over again, one crisis after another.

By this time I had read and reread my now favorite self-help book, *Setting Boundaries with your Adult*

94

Children, by Allison Bottke. I suggest every parent read this book if you have an adult child with any kind of dependency issue. The first time I began reading it, I felt it was too dramatic for me—my son was not as "bad" as the son in the preface—but boy, was I wrong! The book spelled out for me how I enable, why I enable, and my shortcomings (even though, at the time, I thought I was being loving—ugh). I read the book in one sitting the first time. It was like the book was written for me, especially chapter four, "But Deep Down He's Really a Good Kid." I was still treating my son like he was the same kid from long ago, the way I chose to remember him—not the person he was in reality. What an eye-opener for me!

The serenity prayer, which I thought was only for addicts, became ingrained in my mind. If you think of that prayer sentence by sentence and understand what it means with each sentence, it is really powerful. I use that prayer all the time now, not just in dealing with my son. I use it to deal with my husband, too!

This time around with my son, I decided I would try the "helping not enabling" ethic, the loving him without doing for him. I did that for maybe a month, and he quickly slipped down the slippery slope of "help me, Mom!" Once again, he was living with friends, crashing on sofas, and—my guess—using to kill the pain. I realized I couldn't watch this happen. I stuck to my guns, but I was dying inside. My heart was breaking. I was not good at home with my husband and step daughter. Everyone was suffering. This time it had to stop. *I* had to stop.

One day, out of the blue my son called. He was crying and agreed to anything we wanted him to do, go anywhere we wanted him to go. He had been sleeping in alleyways, carrying all his belongings; he'd lost his laptop, clothes, and Bible. I remember that day vividly. It was raining pretty hard, and he gave me directions to an undesirable part of town. I was driving down the road, windshield wipers splashing water out of the way just as fast as it appeared. I was sitting hunched forward, eyes strained to catch a glimpse of my son. I passed a haunting figure standing in the rain, tall, hood over his head, dark clothes, shoes unlaced, smoking. I had to circle back to make sure. It was Patrick. I honked, smiled at him, and realized he was...*dying*. He is six-foot-five, muscular, and very handsome. This guy was tall and gaunt, unshaven, dirty, and smelly, with yellow teeth and yellow fingertips with fingernails bitten to the quick. He smiled at me and said, "Thanks, Mom"...and suddenly he was my little boy all over again.

This time, I recognized my weakness. I also realized that Patrick truly would die if he didn't have help. (I am a believer in the saying about addicts that don't get help: they will eventually die or go to jail). Before I picked Patrick up, I'd spoken with our therapist, who suggested a consultant—similar to an educational consultant—to evaluate Patrick and find somewhere for him to get help on a long-term basis. I brought my son home and fed him. He slept for hours on end. The next morning we held a quasi intervention. The consultant and my son's biological father came and sat with Patrick, my husband and I to discuss the situation.

We picked a twelve-month program in Arizona. It was costly and would be a financial burden. I was grateful to my husband, who had put up with all this chaos for so long. We made it clear to Patrick that this was it—the very last time. He left a couple days later. We didn't really get the full extent of his drug use until a few months later.

The fact that Patrick was across the country was like starting a new life for me. I knew he was in good hands and someone was watching over him, doing all the dirty work that I couldn't seem to do. We had some touch-and-go situations; he ran away three times, used while he was on the run, and had to start over each time. The great thing was that I wasn't involved in any way. I wasn't responsible. It wasn't my fault. He was fucking up on his own without any help from me!

While he was gone, I continued my reading, my support group, and my individual sessions. Without my son under my nose, I felt myself growing by leaps and bounds. I felt liberated. I picked up this little pamphlet, "The Power of Praying for your Adult Children," and read a section every morning. If you are

Christian, this is a wonderful, wonderful book. I keep it in my purse. This little pamphlet and the setting boundaries book have little stickies on almost every page, highlighting those little pearls of wisdom that sometimes I need so badly.

The rehab in Arizona involved the entire family in its healing process. In one of the workshops, which I attended alone (without my husband) I was worried I would succumb to my son's manipulations and brought all my books with me. They kept me strong day after day. I realized I could stay true to me and also love my son. One afternoon when he and I were alone, he asked me to get him a new laptop. I calmly said, "I'm not going to do that," and changed the subject. Patrick became relentless. I was driving on the highway and immediately pulled over to the shoulder and stopped. I looked straight at him and said, "I will gladly take you back if you continue to badger me about this laptop."

YAY! I did it!

Patrick looked at me and quickly said, "OK, OK. I just want to be with you." That was the end of the laptop story. It was so easy. Why hadn't I been able to do that kind of thing before? Because I needed help. That little success propelled me into a forward motion that continues today. I can say no without arguing and mean it.

While my son was in Arizona, I read another book that was recommended to me, *The Lost Years: Surviving a Mother's and Daughter's Worst Nightmare*. This book actually described the ideal model for a parent trying to navigate through a child's addiction. I felt if the mother in this book could do it, so could I!

My son was a "late bloomer" and graduated from his rehab fifteen months later. But he finished the program, and they invited him to intern for six months, before a possible job offer. They considered him one of the harder cases and thought he would be a valuable asset during those times when future residents might be in the same situation.

After the six months, they offered him a job. At times, when we spoke to him on the phone, we felt that old feeling of his ego kicking in—things were going well, and he reverted back to his entitlement and know-it-all attitude. And sure enough after a couple months, he was let go for insubordination. That little old authority nugget that he just thought didn't apply to him. Boy, we'd thought all the worry was behind us.

We worried he was going to use. We worried he would be homeless in Arizona, but we didn't step in to help. He found his way to Prescott, Arizona, a little mecca of recovery. There he found a job, lost it, and found another. My son had ups and downs. He continued to have one crisis after another. Sometimes he would go days without eating and would pass out on the sidewalk. During these times, I avoided talking to him on the phone—to protect myself—and my husband helped him think things through. Together they found the soup kitchen, where to go for jobs, and occasionally we paid for a hotel room in between places to live. We didn't give advice without him asking, and when he began to complain, we would acknowledge the situation and then change the subject. The more we did it, the easier it came.

Then one day I had an epiphany! I'd thought through all these years that if I didn't help my son, he would commit suicide. But he was alive! He'd had many chances to kill himself; we'd said no so many times, and he was still here. Wow—it hit me like a ton of bricks the hold he had on me.

I remember thinking, *if I don't help him, no one will.* Then suddenly, I realized, *What if I died today? He would be thrust into this situation immediately. He is younger than I am, and I will probably die before him.* Patrick was thirty years old. If we continued on till he was fifty or sixty, and then I died, what then? There were so many eye-openers when my eyes were open!

I'm sitting here now thinking back over the years. I remember praying, years of the same request, fervently asking for help to relieve my pain—and now I realize I needed to do it for myself. I prayed for my son—*please, please, help my son*—but Patrick had to do it for himself. God has given me all the abilities to help my son, but I don't have the ability to change him. God has given my son these same abilities—the ability to help himself but not the ability to change me or anyone else. He and I must use what God gave us for ourselves.

These things I know for sure:

Change comes slowly with patience and perseverance.

Sometimes you have to live through the mud to get out of the hole.

Do everything you can and then let it go.

With help, I am now able to see what I couldn't see before, do what I couldn't do before, and live a life that I didn't think I could live before. I have learned to live above what remains to be sad and often trying circumstances.

We are going to visit my son for Thanksgiving this year. It's in a couple of weeks. He has a new job: co-founder of a sober-living, transitional residential home in Prescott. He is broke, doesn't have a car and we hardly hear from him. He feels blessed that he continues to have these opportunities and no longer asks us for anything. I have a care package I'm bringing along with me:-a pair of gloves, the book Renewal, candy, winter slippers and various other items, items I would bring along to a "normal" son when visiting. We don't give Patrick money, although we do still purchase his medication through the pharmacy every month. Helping not enabling, that's the motto I live by today.

Susan

Recommended Reading:
Addictive Thinking, Abraham J. Twerski, M.D.
Facing CoDependence, Pia Melody
Getting Your Loved One Sober: Alternatives to Nagging, Pleading, and Threatening, Robert J. Meyers, Ph.D and Brenda L. Wolfe, Ph.D
Living with Joy, Sanaya Roman
Setting Boundaries with Your Adult Children, Allison Bottke
Sharing Experience Strength and Hope, NarAnon Family Groups
The Lost Years, Kristina Wandzilak, Constance Curry
The Power of Praying for Your Adult Children, Stormie Omartian

Rejoice in hope,
be patient in tribulation,
be consistent in prayer.
Romans 12:12

RYAN

CHILDHOOD

RYAN WAS THE OLDEST of two sons. Their dad and I got divorced when he was two and a half years old. The first two years after the divorce their father visited with them briefly on two occasions. After moving in with his girlfriend, he began to spend more time with them.

Ryan was an intelligent little boy. After being tested prior to entering grade school, he was placed in the gifted program. In the lower grades his teachers always spoke highly of him. He attended church every Sunday and became an acolyte. He would wear a robe and light the candles. He looked like an *angel*.

When Ryan was eight, his dad remarried and moved five hours away. He requested to have his sons spend their summers with him. Although I opposed this arrangement, the boys did spend several summers with their dad and stepmother. When Ryan was in fourth grade, I remarried. It was shortly after the marriage that Ryan began to act up in school and was kicked out of the gifted program. I had him seen by a psychologist on several occasions when he became uncooperative. In reflection, I wish I had tried another psychologist, but instead I just let it go.

Ryan did not get along well with his stepdad, and I reacted in a typical fashion by overcompensating. I felt sorry for him and failed to provide him with the proper discipline. As he got older, his grades fell, and I knew he was not working up to his ability. However, he did engage in several outside activities. He played soccer for eight seasons with his stepdad as his coach, and joined Cub Scouts where I was co-leader. He played baseball for a season but did not like the constructive criticism he received, especially if it was from his stepdad. What he enjoyed the most was biking. One summer he would ride five miles to and from the BMX track where he and a friend would race. When he was fourteen, I had another son. Ryan received him well and liked having another brother.

HIGH-SCHOOL YEARS

AWAY FROM SCHOOL, RYAN was a hard worker and took a job delivering newspapers for several years.

Every Sunday morning I would take him on his route, to the donut shop, and then to church. At fifteen he began to work at a local restaurant. It was after he got his driver's license that he began to break curfews. Instead of reprimanding him, I would just wait up, continually looking out the window, until he came home. It was also during this time that I began to notice a consistent depression about him and became very concerned about his emotional wellbeing. I just wanted him to be happy. I thought he had everything going for him: intelligence, nice looks, and girlfriends, but the problems began with a horrible mess of his bedroom and extended to unsavory friends, fights in and out of school, and incidents requiring involvement from the local law enforcement. Ryan and a friend decided to climb an electrical tower and were brought home by the police. He was also charged with insurance fraud; his truck was not running properly so he insisted it was stolen, this being the second time he claimed a stolen vehicle. He later told me that his friend had taken it and driven it over a cliff. I found him legal counsel that was able to get him off with only a fine. To his credit he did pay the attorney fees and fine himself.

Before long Ryan became a masterful manipulator, telling one lie after another. I believed every last one. He barely graduated from high school and was required to take a summer class through the community college in order receive his diploma. During that summer he decided to go to the community college to become an airplane pilot. After starting college he began to take flying lessons—in reflection, how scary was that! He was required to take a drug test, and even though his behavior was erratic he passed; once more I felt he was just depressed. At the time I did not know how easy it was to get around the drug testing. I had never been around addicts or alcoholics; therefore, I was quite naïve.

To my relief Ryan decided to stop the flying lessons and go into carpentry. At age seventeen he started working for a carpenter during the summer and on weekends, which enabled him to get into the carpenters' union. I thought everything was getting back on track. He had a good job and seemed headed in the right direction. Since his life seemed to be in order, my husband and I agreed to cosign for a truck. Shortly thereafter there were times when he lost his license, but he just drove without it in order to get to work. If his truck was broken down, I would allow him to drive our car to work. I was so convinced that he had to keep his job that I allowed this against my better judgment.

Before too long when Ryan would come home, on occasion he would start shaking and be unable to catch his breath. We called the paramedics. I thought he was having an emotional breakdown or drinking too much; it couldn't be drugs because he had passed several drug tests he had taken for the union. The paramedics took him to the hospital where he was kept overnight and released the next day. By this time he was eighteen, but because of the newly passed Privacy Act and his age, it was never revealed to us that his problems were drug related. I still cannot believe, that under these circumstances, such vital information could have been kept from us. Once, during one of these emergency admissions, a nurse told both his girlfriend and me that he had a personality defect and would never change, advising the girlfriend to break up with him. I will never forget the nurse saying he would never change. A professional should never express such discouraging words. I wish I could go back and tell her we should never give up on anyone, that there is always hope.

REHAB ATTEMPTS

RYAN CONTINUED TO WORK, doing well at his job. One day his supervisor drove him home and told us he felt Ryan would be good supervisory material. After about a year Ryan came home one day and told me he was going to admit himself into rehabilitation for cocaine addiction. This was the first time I finally realized he was taking drugs. I thought to myself, *OK, you do rehab, straighten out, and then you can move on with your life*—just that simple. Little did we know how long and very hard this journey was going to be.

Ryan's stepdad and I told him we would support him financially while he was in rehab. He lasted one week and quit. We told him he had a choice: either return to rehab or move out. He chose to leave. He had been gone for several months when he told us he wanted to try rehab again and asked if he could return home. Over the next several years I lost count of how many inpatient and outpatient facilities and halfway houses he entered. He never completed a program. Once I drove him to a program in Cleveland where he stayed one day and found a ride home. Once he tried a methadone treatment program but had to quit as it became too expensive for him.

On several occasions Ryan was arrested. When this happened, I actually felt relieved. I felt that being incarcerated would give him a chance to improve and get back on track. However, he would only remain in prison for several months before being released due to overcrowding. While in prison he always did everything required in order to get out, including regular AA meetings, but he was far from being ready to change. He would come home and steal from us: money, jewelry, debit cards, anything of value. He would even steal from his little brother. We eventually bought a safe to lock our valuables in, and I would carry my purse with me from room to room if he was in our home.

At one point Ryan got his own apartment. I was excited and hopeful. My mother took him shopping and bought him a new sofa, and I also assisted in getting what he needed. His girlfriend moved in with him. His neighbors, an elderly couple, told me how much of a gentleman he was and how he was helpful to them. It was only several months before things began to fall apart; his girlfriend moved out, and he was unable to pay his rent. He was evicted.

He threatened suicide five times. Each time I took him to the hospital, where he was admitted. I found the hospital would only admit him if he was proven to be a threat to himself or someone else. With this knowledge I learned to lie to try to find him the help he so badly needed. But with each attempt he was out in two or three days. While in the hospital, he would call continually all day, complaining of what a terrible mother I was and asking how I could do this to him. I would have stopped answering the phone, but it was just after my father had died and my mother was in poor health, so I felt I needed to answer the calls. We finally got caller ID. I also had a cell phone at the time, and it seemed every time I left the house, just to get away, Ryan would call; there was no escaping. When the phone rang, I wanted to run and hide; eventually I got rid of my cell phone.

When Ryan was no longer living with us, he would sometimes come to the house, knock relentlessly, and cause a scene until we let him in. When I insisted he leave, he would block the door, follow me from room to room, and become loud and out of control. We felt compelled to give him money just to get him out of the house. His little brother was so frightened he would run and hide in his bedroom.

One week he called every night in middle of the night pleading for me to come and pick him up. On one occasion he borrowed his brother's car and could not remember where in town he had parked it. He called and asked me to come and get him; I refused, but somehow he found his way back to the house.

My husband was in the Reserves and had to be gone two weeks several times out of every year. He actually signed up to go away more often than required in order to escape the chaos within his home. We had all become victims of Ryan's addiction.

MY TURNING POINT

BEFORE TOO LONG, AFTER being alone for two weeks, I found myself unable to sleep or eat. I paced constantly around our home. I had lost thirty-nine pounds in one month's time. A friend of mine, who was a nurse, talked to me one day and said I needed to seek counseling for myself. I knew she was right. I was feeling desperate and without hope. I felt a strong need to open up and put an end to all the false pretentions. I knew I must change for the sake of my family; how unfair it was for them to live in such a chaotic environment! My youngest son had seen more by the time he was seven than most kids experience in a lifetime. He had witnessed his brother curled up in a ball in the corner of a room and totally out of control. He had seen Ryan being taken from his home by the police in handcuffs. He had learned how to hide his money and treasures in a locked box. When his brother entered the house, he would run to his room and lock the door. Why should he have to live like this? My younger son gave me the reason and the strength to make a change. Also, I could no longer allow Ryan to be in our home while using; in doing so I began to realize I would be enabling him. If he should die from his addiction, I had to know I did nothing that would have allowed it to happen.

The violent behavior continued when Ryan was in need of his drugs. At one point he had his stepdad by the throat. I feared for my husband's life and knew I must get a restraining order against my son. With the support of the POTADA group, Parents of Teenage Alcoholics and Drug Abusers, I went to the courthouse, crying the whole time, and obtained a PFA against my son for one year. On several occasions I weakened and allowed him in. He sometimes told me he wanted to go to the hospital and be admitted, but when we got there he changed his mind, grabbed my purse for money, and ran. I even had to stop a policeman once to get Ryan out of my car and then go to the police station to file a report.

My husband and I eventually decided to purchase a security system, informing Ryan that the police would come should he try to force his way into our home. This was one more step I had to take; I was so sad at the reality of taking this action. This was never how I saw my life going. *After all, we are provided with the God-given instincts to provide for, protect, and defend our children; these are essential to our parenting. How could it be possible that I must now protect myself from my child?*

Once when Ryan agreed to go into rehab, we met with one of the women who worked there who pulled some strings to have him admitted. One of the requirements for his admission was that he needed to be high. To make this possible I had to take him that evening to buy him drugs off the street in order for him to be high the next day when I took him to the facility. This was one of the most horrible things I had to do. I felt like I was putting my life in danger, but what choice did I have? I was learning many things about how the system worked, a system that so badly needed improvement. We were often put into a position of having to do these horrible things, and each time I would ask myself, *how many more times must I do this?* But I could not give up. I just kept going, trying to deal with this lifestyle I'd never chosen.

I also got to the point where I found the strength not to bail Ryan out of jail when arrested and requested that the rest of our family not bail him out either, but his paternal grandmother did. I became very angry with her. I felt if I, his mother, had finally gotten enough strength to do a very hard thing, then everyone else should be able to as well. Since then I have learned that everyone gets to that point in his or her own time. But I still felt resentment. After all, he could not go to her home, as his grandfather was ill, so where else could he go? A cab dropped him off at our house in middle of the night. Because my husband was trying to sleep and had to get up for work in several hours, it was just easier to let Ryan in. So, there we were again. It is most important to have the whole family on the same page, but can be a very difficult process in getting there.

Ryan eventually totaled his truck, and because we had cosigned we had to pay it off: another lesson learned. The positive outcome from this was he no longer had anything to drive, which alleviated our worry that he would put himself or someone else in danger by driving while under the influence of drugs or alcohol.

One of the most important things I learned going to Al-Anon and POTADA was "Say what you mean, mean what you say, and don't say it mean." This became my motto in life. Also, someone compared the addict's recovery to that of a cancer patient's treatment to help me understand how important it is for addicts to have to pay their consequences. It was just like a cancer patient's chemotherapy. Even though it was destroying their body, they knew they must go through it to get rid of the cancer. In the case of addiction, addicts must pay the consequences that will hopefully help them to reach their rock bottom. I felt like Ryan had hit his rock bottom several times, but it was never enough. There were several times when he lived with other addicts or slept under a bridge. He lost his job, lost his girlfriend, lost his home, and had spent months in jail. What would it take for him to reach rock bottom?

I finally came to understand that Ryan used drugs as medication. He was never happy and thought drugs would fill the void. He eventually moved from cocaine to heroin. One time when I was talking to him I looked into his eyes, and it felt as if I was looking into the eyes of Satan. He was no longer the son I knew. I feel that putting drugs into your body was like taking Satan into your soul. It was a terrifying moment. I had to grieve losing the son I thought he was and somehow start accepting him as he was, addiction and all. I loved my son but hated the addiction.

There were so many times I found myself on my knees crying out to God to take care of Ryan. I knew that He loved him even more than I did, and that Ryan was in better hands with God than with me. I could do no more. I had tried everything. Another motto from Al Anon I took on was, "Let go and let God." This helped me through many nights. It was amazing how many times things began to work out without my involvement and how many times God put someone

I needed in my path. One time I remember so well, I was praying for Ryan and feeling very despondent when a man came to our house to replace a broken window in Ryan's vehicle. This was supposed to be taken care of at a gas station up the street but due to a miscommunication this repairman came to our home. We ended up talking, and he told me his name was Ryan. He said he was a recovering drug addict and offered me hope. He gave me a hug and let me cry. He left me with his phone number and told me to call him whenever I needed to talk. I felt he had definitely been sent to me for a reason. There had been so many times that God protected Ryan from very dangerous situations. I became convinced that I should never stop praying or give up hope.

RYAN'S RECOVERY

Eventually Ryan became homeless and needed a place to live. He was also being threatened by drug dealers and became paranoid, feeling like people were following him. My mother felt sorry for him and decided to take him into her home. She was in poor health, and despite his addiction he helped to take care of her. She died after several months, and after her death Ryan cashed some of her checks. I was notified about the bad checks, as my name was also on them, and I turned Ryan into the local authorities. I did not press charges but told him I would if he did not get help. At this point he had burned all his bridges and lost his friends.

During a sober period he had met a nice girl who decided to take him in. She was in her last semester of college and became pregnant. Even this was not enough to change his behavior. He ended up stealing a woman's purse and got arrested. This time no one posted bail. I did not talk to him for the first three months he was in jail. I was angry. I had never raised him to sink to this depth. I decided to go to the hearing, and the guard allowed me to give him a hug before taking him away. He was sentenced to five years. He served two and a half in jail and the remaining two and a half on probation. I knew what hell I had been through when I realized I was OK with his incarceration. At least he was safe.

And this time would prove to be different. Every other time Ryan had been in jail, he'd done what was necessary to get released, but this time he decided to do what he could to get better. He was accepted into the HOPE Program, to which one is required to apply. They had their own pod in the jail where they were safe. They had to follow all of the rules or they would be expelled. It was a Christian-based program where daily, for three months, there were Bible studies and drug-rehabilitation programs. Ryan actually accepted Christ through this program and started teaching Bible studies. After one year he was transferred to a prison, where he became involved in a carpentry program and even taught some classes while still attending church and Bible studies. However, our relationship remained strained and needed much healing on both sides.

About one year before Ryan's release, I became very nervous. I was so afraid that once he got out he would revert back to his addiction. It was at this point I found SOS, a therapist-facilitated group of individuals who were dealing with addiction within their families. Once more I found the support I needed to stay strong. When the time came for Ryan's release, he was able to line up a job working as a carpenter and arranged to live with his paternal grandmother. There was that part of me that wished I could have allowed him to come home, but I knew it would not be in our best interest. Since he did not have a license for the first year, I would drive him to his first few NA meetings. I also took him to meet with his probation officer weekly for one year. This became our opportunity to talk and spend time with one another. This was my choice, and I felt comfortable with it.

Ryan has now been out of prison for five years and drug free for almost seven years. He joined a church and attends on a regular basis. He lives with his girlfriend and their son, who is now six. Two years ago he started his own business and is doing well. He was an assistant coach on his son's t-ball team and attends his son's practices and games. He has had to work hard to get to this point and is still dealing with some of the consequences of his addiction but is definitely heading in the right direction. With each clean year under his belt, I feel more confident in his recovery. I also realize in the event of a relapse it is his responsibility to take the steps to get back on track. I feel the best chance any addict has is turning to their God and working the twelve-step program. I also feel the best advice I have ever received is not to do something for an addict that they can do for themselves. If someone is in rehab and doing what they need to do, then support them, not necessarily financially but emotionally; and as difficult as it is, if they are not accepting of treatment, we must step back and get out of their way.

There is something positive that has evolved from this experience. My relationship with God has grown to a level it would never have reached had this not been a part of my life. I have learned what faith means to me and how it has played out in my existence. I am always willing to talk to other people going through a similar experience so that I may provide them with hope and some wisdom.

My youngest son is now eighteen and has given his life to Christ. I do think because of going through all that he has, he has chosen this direction. He has started college to become an architect and would also like to be a group leader. He works at a Christian camp where he hopes to be a counselor and eventually the worship leader. Who would have ever guessed that out of all this chaos and trauma, this is where we would be today? I know it is through God that we are where we are now.

Ryan, 33, resides in Pittsburgh with his wife and two children. He has maintained sobriety for seven years and operates his own business.

Pam

Chris Wolf, M.S.

MANY YEARS AGO MY neighbor recognized from my behavior that I was dealing with a family member's addiction. She encouraged me to attend an Al Anon meeting. I felt so distressed that I did not even want to open the door to attend. I could have slid under the door easier than open it. But I took her advice and continued to attend the Al-Anon meetings once a week for the next thirteen years. At these meetings I was always interested in how a person's addiction affected the family and what if anything could the family do to be spared from this experience. Several years later I went back to the University of Pennsylvania where I earned my master's degree in counseling and my certification as a family therapist. My primary focus became not only in helping the addict but also in helping the family members affected by a loved one's addiction.

My first job was at a mental health facility in Philadelphia, which did not provide services to family members of addicts. I presented the other therapists working within the clinic with a live sculpture of an addictive system. The aim was to show them that possibly 67% of their clientele came from a family with addiction. It changed the entire facility and our scope of services embraced the importance of working with the families. At the end of my first year, 55% of the clients were family members. I have as many years of experience working with the addicts as I do working with family members. I was of the strong belief we needed to look at the entire family system in order to help one person. If we could help the family members we could get the addict into treatment earlier and prevent the family system from taking on dysfunctional behaviors acquired from living with this disease.

Even though "Hope Never Lost" focuses on the adolescent, I will be using the word child. Some parents may have chosen to read this book with the intention of preventing their child from becoming addicted to a substance or self-destructive behavior. For those, I will touch lightly upon some considerations a parent should take into account when raising their child. These considerations could make a difference when they face the challenges of adolescence. Perhaps you have chosen to read it because you are dealing with a child whose behavior is concerning you regarding the use of drugs or alcohol or a child who is already on a self-destructive path.

My passion has been to stop the addiction *and* stop the generational dysfunction it can create in families. When one person in a family is addicted, it can cause the entire family to get trapped in different ways. This entrapment can become a generational pattern of dysfunctional ways of coping.

UNDERSTANDING ADDICTION

IT IS IMPERATIVE THAT family members understand how the disease of addiction works and how an individual behaves when his or her disease is active. To me, addiction or "trapped behavior" means "powerless." We need to realize that once a person is addicted to something, he or she is caught in a self-defeating, self-destructive cycle of which there is no semblance of control. The person has tried to stop the cycle numerous times, but failed. There is tremendous anxiety at the thought of losing the substance or behavior to which he or she is addicted. I will initially ask addicts, "So, what are you running from?" Most often they will say, "myself." Many express that their drug takes them to a different place, a place, said one person "where no one can reach me. It is a wonderful feeling." What the addict fails to realize is that once the drug wears off, they are right in front of what they escaped. They cannot escape themselves. High or not, wherever they go, they are with them.

While drugs provide instant escape, recovery provides the framework to face adversity and discomfort. It is not unusual for a young adult struggling with addiction to agree to rehab the first time only because there is a person's footprint on their behind. Statistics reveal that at least 90% of individuals are coerced into treatment by family members, the legal system, or by their employers. However, it is their first step in the recovery process. Recovery for the addict occurs in multiple stages and often with setbacks. The recovery also will begin to occur for members of the immediate family. In many cases it is the first opportunity for them to step back and open their eyes to the reality of the dysfunction and chaos with which they have been living.

The life of an addicted person is completely focused on their drug. Addicts depend on this drug to function and feel better. They want access to this drug when they need it and they experience severe anxiety when it is unavailable. Every time the addicted person feels uncomfortable, he or she relies on the drug to feel comfortable again. The comfort wears off when the drug does. All feelings, thoughts, and behaviors are focused on regaining the short-lived state of comfort. Over time, the addict will sell his or her soul, morals, and values to obtain the drug. He will lie, steal, and manipulate others to maintain his drug use. She will threaten and offend others. Parents cannot believe their child would do these things. They slip into denial because the truth is too devastating. This fact can be seen in the previous chapters, each mother went into a denial phase not once but many times through their child's addiction. I know a man whose son has been addicted to drugs since he was a teenager. He is now in his forties. He tells his son, "I love you. You will always have a place in my life and in my home, but your disease is not welcome." When his son is using he knows he will not find support from his father. This man is saying to his son, "You cannot ask me to go with you down the road to self destruction. I love you too much to participate and watch you destroying yourself." This is healthy behavior from the father and helps his son's addiction.

Every addict affects the lives of at least six people. Education and support for these individuals is critical. The experience can become so traumatic that it can later lead to post-traumatic stress disorder. Family members often must seek medical attention to deal with their stress, anxiety and depression. So, what do you do when someone you love has a problem that he or she will not confront? First of all, you do not have to feel powerless.

There are things you can do to get them help and stop the addiction from progressing.

To do what is necessary might challenge you to acquire a new perspective on the reality of your loved one's disease. It may also require you to take some difficult actions in order to help someone who is in addiction or moving in that direction. To be able to recognize what is needed you must take an honest look at what you are doing to help keep the addiction going. The first step is to examine honestly what you are doing to enable your child's addiction. Ask yourself some of these questions:

- Do you do things that are not helpful, like bail your son or daughter out of jail or pay their fines to avoid any consequences? Too often a parent will act out of the fear of their own discomfort resulting from the consequences of their child's behavior.
- When he or she gets a DUI, do you spend hours driving him or her around?
- Does your child emotionally blackmail you?
- Are you afraid of your child's rejection?
- Do you think your actions will alleviate the addict's pain and discomfort?
- Do you think this is an adolescent phase and that the addict will change once they graduate?
- Does your child's behavior create such intense anxiety that you do things against your better judgment?

- Does your fear of what others think of you as a parent dictate your choices?
- Does your addicted child's negative behavior take away time from your other children?
- Does your child's negative behavior give him or her more power than anyone else in the family?

If the family shifts its focus to doing whatever it takes to keep everyone else healthy, it will help the person abusing drugs and alcohol to stop the behavior and seek treatment sooner. It is confusing, isn't it? How could this possibly help? Well it does. Learn how to calm your anxiety so you do not act compulsively in making your decisions. Learn how to handle your discomfort so it does not rule your behavior. Begin to attend a Twelve step program such as Al-Anon or Nar-Anon so you can learn from the experience of others. Your family and you need support to stop the vicious cycle of your lives being dictated by addictive behavior.

I tried to help one father whose son had been in addiction for years. The addict was a bright young man full of promise, but by the time I met him he had a reputation of being the "problem." His family feared his terrible temper, and he had lost the respect of his siblings. I was powerless to help the situation because the father believed it was his parental responsibility to rescue his son and get him out of trouble. He would say, "I just cannot let him go down that road." He was unable to see that his son was going down that road despite his trying to rescue him.

Know the difference between helping and rescuing. As you witnessed from reading the five mothers' chapters, each mother more than once allowed their child to come home before their treatment program was over; each mother would often go along with their child's plan rather than listen to her own better judgment. Addiction forces us to love in a way we might never have imagined. Parents often must bear the emotional pain of enforcing an action upon their child that would be perceived as hurtful or unbearable by others, in order to help their child in the end. This action was also brought out in the previous chapters where grandparents, especially, will try to rescue the child, not understanding the difficult goal of the parent. Addiction is about life and death. We cannot take this disease lightly. Many of our young adults are dying or committing suicide because they do not know what else to do to escape the complete control of addiction.

CONTRIBUTING FACTORS
TO ADDICTIVE BEHAVIOR

THERE IS NO FORMULA which will enable parents to keep their children drug free. However, the following areas have been known to lead to addictive behavior.

There are some individuals who may be predisposed to addiction through chemical imbalances or genetics. Others grow up in homes where there are patterns of explosive anger by an actively addicted parent. Such havoc creates a tenuous environment, like walking on a minefield. The family never knows whether or not a bomb is going to explode. The children may turn to a drug or alcohol to calm anxiety. And then the addiction cycle begins for them as their reliance grows. People can unconsciously use drugs to medicate a pre-existing condition such as Attention Deficit Disorder, Depression, or Bi-Polar. It is important to properly assess the condition. Psychotropic drugs are available for these conditions. I had a recovering alcoholic evaluated for ADHD. He called me from the waiting room of the clinic during the evaluation. In filling out the questionnaire he said, "This makes sense of my entire life." He was so relieved. Many of my patients have told me their addiction began as a way to escape the trauma of being bullied, a humiliating experience in front of peers or the memory of a traumatic event, such as the death of a parent or friend. Knowing this, parents need to help their children learn how to deal with the trials of life in a healthy way in order to prevent one harmful experience from changing the rest of their lives. There are healthy ways we can learn from these trials and use them to make us into deeper and more compassionate human beings.

I believe in today's society parents have less control over their children and the unexpected events in life that may scar them. I am grateful I am not a teenager or a parent of a teenager at this time in our history. Both have been confronted with a new set of challenges brought forth by social media and technology. Never before has there been such instant gratification in so many areas—television, personal cell phones, texting, video games, movies, and computers. Toys for young children now have computer chips, the toy interacts and even talks to them. Most children grow up expecting to be entertained, which can result in their inability to deal with boredom. *They have not learned how to sit with discomfort* but rather learn at an early age there is a remedy for everything. Television often gives them their standard on how to act and dress. They are influenced by the sexual behavior seen in movies and television. Through computers and personal tablets, which many children now receive by the time they are in third and fourth grade, they are exposed to a world from which there is very little protection. This world consists of pornography, sexual predators, scams and yes, a world accessing our youth to drugs and alcohol. With such high accessibility to drugs and alcohol, be it on the internet, at school, or an after-school job, there is no formula which will enable parents to totally safe guard their children from the world of drugs.

PERSONAL REFLECTIONS ON
PARENTING SKILLS

MANY OF YOU READING this book could be described as super responsible parents. You are trying to do your job 100%. Our culture suggests that if you create a perfect home for your children, they will mature to become healthy, happy people. Not so. If you were going to be held responsible for what kind of adult your child becomes, then you would have been given a blueprint and remote control at birth. You cannot monitor or control what your child says or does once he or she leaves your house. You can influence them, provide a model of values and behavior, but you cannot control their destiny. There is a plan and purpose for his or her life that is none of our business. Or children came here to learn certain things and we need to get out of the way of those lessons.

THIS IS IMPORTANT! Please absorb this concept! Over responsible parents create under responsible children. If a parent is always rushing in to help or do something for their child -- something the child needs to learn for him or herself – this is what the child begins to believe: "You don't think I can do it." It undermines their confidence in their own ability and sense of accomplishment. Give them time to struggle with a task. It will provide them with the experience and satisfaction of reaching a goal.

Your job as a parent is to help your children acquire the skills they are going to need to navigate through life by the time they graduate from high school. You need to learn from watching the animal world. In the world of animals, their natural instinct tells them if they do not prepare their offspring, they may not survive. We need to have the same attitude. We seem to think that when our children grow up they will all of a sudden have all the skills they need in adulthood. What are these skills? Your teenagers are going through a challenging life stage transition. They are leaving childhood, which is obedience and following instruction, into adulthood. In adulthood they will be navigating their own life. They will need to gain the skills of being self-supportive, providing for their own food and shelter. They must also have good interpersonal skills and know the value of honest relationships. What skills do they need to be able to achieve this? In everything you do as a parent ask yourself, "What am I teaching, and is this teaching my children the skills they require?" Children just do not grow up in a protective environment and then at a certain age have all the skills they need to make it on their own. The family needs to be a place where they feel safe enough to ask any question and express their personal feelings without the feeling of rejection, inadequacy or humiliation.

What kind of self-esteem does your child have? It is an inside job. I could have one hundred people surround you and tell you they think you are great, and it would not matter; if you do not believe it, you will not allow for the information to enter. All we need to do to feel inferior is set a standard and convince ourselves we cannot reach it.

We need to give our children a way to look at life that supports them through the difficult trials and situations. Let us use bullying as an example. Some children are taught there is purpose to this trial. What is bullying teaching you? How is this being used to strengthen you inside and make you into a stronger, deeper and more authentic person? What are you learning from the trial? What skills are you acquiring from this experience that you will be able to use the rest of your life? Many are taught to believe God never gives them something they cannot handle, and with it He will provide a means of escape. We need to help our children surf life and be able to stay afloat when a wave hits. We all know people who are never the same after a traumatic experience. I am of the personal belief it is not of the higher will for anyone to have their life permanently changed by trauma. As adults, most of us would say it was the most difficult times in our lives that were the most fruitful even though they were painful at the time. How do we get through problems? Have you ever discussed dealing with conflict and problems with your child?

As parents, we need to teach our children how to withstand discomfort and recognize the importance of experiencing this at a young age. There is no formula to insure your child will not use drugs, but this one thing could be a major factor in drug-proofing your child's future. What does it mean to learn to withstand discomfort? Say your child of 4 years wants you to buy him something they see in a store. You don't want to, and he becomes so upset you give in just to stop him from crying or yelling. You have just passed up an opportunity to teach your child to deal with discomfort, the discomfort of not having what he wants. If you stay calm, yet firm, and let them discover that "no" means "no" he will be learning to deal with the discomfort he feels within his body. He will be learning that acting that way does not get him what he wants. If this is difficult for you to do, then you need to deal with the discomfort or anxiety *you* feel. What happens very often is that parents give in to their child to relieve their own discomfort. It is learning to deal with discomfort on our way to reaching a goal that gives us a strong will and the confidence we can do it.

The need to be liked by their peers and included into a group is supposedly the greatest need of adolescents. It is stronger than their need to obey their parents. The emphasis is on *conformity* rather than *uniqueness.* Adolescents spend too much energy trying to look like and act like everyone else so they will not be rejected. I believe we need to help our children look for how they are different rather than try to be like everyone else. No one has the same fingerprints as anyone else. We need to help our children discover the many ways they are different. It is our differences that provide us with the qualities we will contribute to the world. Let them know there is no one else in the world exactly like them.

We also need to teach our children how to recognize their own inner guidance. There is a way our body signals us a strong "yes" and a strong "no". We have constant inner guidance available to help us navigate safely in the world. Some refer to this inner guidance as their "gut" feeling. This is because we are given this guidance in the solar plexus of our body. It is important we teach our children how to listen to this guidance and how to use it to make choices in life. We can ask ourselves any question that can be answered "yes" and "no" and notice that the solar plexus tightens for a "no" and relaxes for a "yes". You can practice with yourself. Ask yourself questions that you know are "no" and have some emotion to them. Listen quickly before your head gets involved. The head mainly contributes fear. You will not be guided by your soul or higher power through fear. There is no need to frighten or paralyze yourself. How will this help you to take care of yourself? Fear is a strong emotion that not only controls us but is used to control one another.

All these ideas bring us to a point of realization. Do you know these things? Do you apply them to your own life? How can you teach your children what you don't know? Take the time to learn how to listen to your inner guidance so you can teach it to your children. Learn how to use your own emotions to alert you as to how situations and people are affecting you, and then you will be able to teach it to your children. Take the time to go inside and get to know how you are different from others; allow yourself to be different. This will allow your child to value and embrace his or her individuality and not anesthetize who they are through drugs and alcohol.

JILL FINE, M.S. ED.

"HOW ARE YOU?"

I've asked thousands of people that question over years of working with addicts, alcoholics, and their loved ones. I ask out of genuine curiosity and out of the desire to encourage people to talk about how they are feeling. It can be very healing.

The addicts' and alcoholics' responses vary according to where they are in their recovery. The families' responses are almost always the same. They are dumbfounded that I am asking how THEY are. No one has asked THEM for a really long time. And it doesn't seem to matter to them how they are. What matters is how their addict is and what they, the family, can do to help, alter, fix, and cure this person. The families, too, want to tell me all about the addict. There is a bottomless pit of stories of deceit, dishonesty, and degradation. They want to tell them and tell them and tell them. They are exhausted from experiencing the pain over and over again, and yet they go on telling.

The greatest challenges I have faced in working with families and loved ones of addicts and alcoholics are enlightening them to the reality there is very little, if anything, they can do to help, alter, fix, or cure the addict, and convincing them that they need to get help for themselves. It is obvious to them the addict needs help, but not so obvious that they also need help. This help ranges from education about the disease of addiction, treatment, and recovery processes to individual therapy and support from other families in similar crises. Families are told to focus their attention, time, energy, and love on themselves rather than the addict. They are told to recognize the effects the disease has had on them and to seek help for their own recovery process. For many this is a seemingly impossible task.

It is a cliché, but a true one: an addict has to want to get help in order for him or her to seek treatment. The family can learn about enabling, which is basically any behavior that makes it easier for the chemically dependent person to continue to use drugs or alcohol. When enabling stops, there is a greater possibility of the addict reaching enough of a bottom to seek help. This is only a possibility, not a guarantee. The family can learn about behaviors they need to change in order to support a newly sober alcoholic, but once more with no guarantees. However, the more a family member learns and changes, the greater chance the addict has of a successful recovery. The more family members learn how to detach, the greater chance they have of a successful recovery.

Detachment is a concept with which families struggle. They think it means having no contact or disowning the addict, not caring anymore. Many tell me, "I will never kick my child out of the house." The truth is, detachment means none of these things. Rather, with love, detachment means continuing to love the addict but hating the disease and all of its splatter. It means establishing boundaries, rules, and limitations and protecting oneself from the physical, financial, legal, social, emotional, and spiritual effects of addiction. For families, it means learning to let go of the need for control and focusing attention on themselves and what they need to change in order to be happier and at peace.

The challenges often begin before the addict even enters treatment. Denial kicks in at almost the same time as drug and alcohol abuse begins. "He is just going through a normal teenage phase." "It's only marijuana." "She has a lot of pain and needs medication." "He is under a lot of stress at work, and drinking helps him to relax." As the disease progresses, living with it becomes predictably unpredictable. Families find themselves unconsciously adapting to the addict, adjusting their behavior, and thinking in unhealthy ways in order to coexist with this person. Families require education in detachment in order to maintain their health and to create even the possibility of the addict getting help. If the addict seeks treatment, families experience relief and believe that if the addict gets help, everything will be OK. Unfortunately, this is not usually the case. Sending an addict back home to a family that has not changed almost inevitably will result in relapse. Families do not understand that it is not enough for just the addict to get help.

I worked in an agency where we had family treatment weekly, and it always amazed and disappointed me how few family members were interested in participating. When they were contacted, their belief was that the addict was the one with the problem. "Why do I have to go to group meetings? The addict needs to get better, not me."

So how do you tell someone that he or she, as someone who loves an addict, has become as sick, sometimes sicker than the addict? Family members will tell you they are having trouble concentrating at work, that their heart races, that they have gastrointestinal problems and high blood pressure, that they've develop ulcers and cannot sleep. They confess to hiding from friends and other family members out of shame and are obsessive about what they can do to help their addict get well. They are hopeless and depressed. One mother with whom I worked was admitted to the emergency room twice believing she was having a heart attack. The diagnosis was panic and anxiety.

So family members have physical ailments directly connected to their constant stress levels, but they do not necessarily connect them to living with addiction. They have mental limitations—they are confused and have constant distractions and obsessive thoughts combined with compulsive behaviors. "Maybe if I keep dumping his alcohol down the sink, he won't drink so much." An eighty-two-year-old father put himself in grave danger by going to a crack house to try to drag his son out. This is the insane thinking and behavior of being in a relationship with an addict. Family members suffer greatly emotionally and spiritually and often become depressed and fearful due to the ongoing trauma to which they are subjected. Parents feel tremendous guilt, believing there is something they did that contributed to their child's addiction or something they could do to make it better. They feel shame. Even though families today are educated about addiction as a disease that is not the addict's fault, society continues to judge addicts harshly, and families carry the brunt of those judgments. So they hide and lie. "He has the flu and is unable to attend the family reunion." Lying compromises their moral and spiritual values, and they are caught in the vicious cycle of addiction. Do the behavior, feel the shame about it, and repeat the behavior to get rid of the shame.

And then there is the anger that is present in every loved one with whom I have worked. The anger ranges from chronic resentment to full-blown rage. The anger is deep and powerful and so very hard to manage. It manifests itself in a variety of self-destructive behaviors, which, over time, can result in major health issues. It also results in behaviors that do not promote healthy recovery for the addict.

Families' spiritual values and connections are conflicted and/or lost when dealing with addiction. "How could God let this happen?" they wonder. Spiritual principles such as gratitude, faith, honesty, service to others, humility, and acceptance are lost. Spiritual practices, whether performed in a place of worship or elsewhere, are sacrificed. And yet they will continue to maintain that the addict is the sick one, not them.

It requires a tremendous amount of compassion, understanding, empathy, and unconditional love to gently encourage and support the "co-addict" to get help. Once he or she crosses that threshold and surrenders to the need to get help, there is no turning back.

That is when miracles start to happen. The process begins with surrender: surrendering to the need for help and surrendering to take suggestions from treatment professionals and others who have been through what they are experiencing.

Acceptance is the next major hurdle for loved ones. Acceptance means that there are limitations in how much they can do to help the addict's recovery and that there will be ups and downs in the process. Acceptance means that relapse is often a part of recovery. Due to the unfortunate chronic nature of addiction, relapse is not unusual for someone's first attempt at recovery, and it is important for families to understand this so they do not panic when it happens.

Families need to change behaviors, like talking about their feelings rather than stifling or denying them. They need to practice tough love and maintain friendships, social activities, and hobbies. If you are a parent with other children, make sure to be paying attention to them, and provide opportunities to process what they are experiencing.

Learning about addiction is necessary to fight this disease. Read addiction literature and the many booklets from twelve-step fellowships. Attend support group meetings and meetings where other families can help you through their knowledge. Attend open meetings of Alcoholics Anonymous or Narcotics Anonymous to hear firsthand the experiences of addiction and recovery. Often in an AA or NA speaker meeting, you will hear addicts or alcoholics tell you exactly what their family did that was helpful and what they did that was enabling. Attend Al Anon and NarAnon to gain insight and support in dealing with this powerful disease.

Another major hurdle for loved ones of addicts is the spiritual principle of forgiveness. This can be a major challenge, as addicts and alcoholics frequently create major problems for those who love them, including legal and financial problems. They will lie, steal, and cheat. "I used to sleep with my purse under my pillow until he stole money right out from under me. Now I keep it locked in my car when he is around." How do you forgive your child for stealing your wedding ring?

It requires courage and faith in a higher power to gain the willingness to forgive. There is a vast amount of literature on forgiveness, but for the purpose of this work, forgiveness is defined as follows:

> The decision to let go of resentment, anger, and thoughts of revenge as a result of a real or perceived offense, hurt, or wrongdoing against you. Forgiving someone does not mean denying a person's responsibility for hurting you, nor does it mean minimizing or justifying the act. It does mean being willing to forgive someone without condoning or excusing what they did, and then letting it go.[1]

Forgiveness takes a lot of time and patience. Forgiveness does not mean condoning the addict's or alcoholic's behavior; it cannot be done for the sake

---

1 Retrieved from http://www.essentiallifeskills.net/forgiveness-and-letting-go.html, 2011.

of the addict, but rather achieving forgiveness must be done for your own sake, so that you can move on. A common theme in recovery communities about resentment is that it is like swallowing poison and expecting the other person to die. Resentment will hurt you. Resentment may sicken you physically, emotionally, and spiritually. Religious communities, twelve-step recovery programs, family support groups, therapy, and counseling provide good resources to work toward forgiveness. Know that your ability to forgive your addict will open the door for the addict to be able to forgive him/herself.

Your physical well-being is critical to have the strength to take the actions necessary for your recovery. Eating properly and getting exercise, rest, relaxation, and sleep are very important for family members. Keep up with your own medical appointments. Laughter is a recovery tool, so have fun and watch funny movies. Spend time with people you enjoy who can help to lighten your load.

As your recovery progresses, you will begin to experience some of the rewards of the journey. You will recognize that somehow the sun manages to come up without your help! You can stop apologizing for what someone else did. You really know and believe that you did not cause the addiction. You can allow other people to be wrong even though you are convinced you can make things better if you had the chance. You stop worrying and start believing that worrying is a useless waste of your time and energy.

SOME DO'S AND DON'TS

DON'T:

- Disqualify, deny, or disguise disrespectful, shameful, or abusive behaviors.
- Lecture, threaten, argue, or nag.
- Cover up the consequences of addiction.
- Give back trust too easily.
- Lose your temper.
- Try to control.
- Feel you always need to be right.
- Expect reliability and constancy in relationships.
- Ignore your own needs.

DO:

- Learn about the disease of addiction. You did not cause it, you cannot control it, and you cannot cure it.
- Learn how to ask for help.
- Get connected to yourself through self-exploration, prayer, and meditation.
- Learn to identify and express your feelings in an appropriate manner.
- Learn how to deal with powerlessness. Use the serenity prayer.

- Stop reacting and living in response to how others are acting.
- Recognize the only person you can control is you.
- Learn how to set boundaries and enforce them.
- Learn how to detach with love—not with anger and indifference.
- Find a family support group, counselor, and/or twelve-step meeting.
- Have fun! Laugh, play games, and engage in fun hobbies and activities.

Accept responsibility for your life regardless of whether or not the addict changes, focusing on your needs, dreams, and desire.

FAMILY SERENITY PRAYER

God, grant me the serenity to accept
the people I cannot change,
The courage to change the person I can,
And the wisdom to know that it's me.

EPILOGUE

AS TEENAGERS, MANY OF us believe ourselves to be immortal and exempt from bad things happening. This thinking is often reflected in the many areas where a teenager will take serious risks from unprotected sex to reckless driving to drug and alcohol abuse. In today's society substance abuse is without doubt the biggest risk teenagers can take and will lead to reckless behavior in every area of their lives. Some teens will become powerless over their addiction even before they graduate. Statistics show that every addict will impact six other lives as a result of their disease. Young adults in addiction are battling for their lives. As the disease progresses to the later stages, they will "sell their soul" and compromise all their values. Learning what you can and cannot control is a large part of the solution.

Our collective conclusion is that we had more power to change than we initially realized. By receiving the education we need and the support to help us change what we believe does not work, we can greatly influence the outcome of addiction in our children's lives. By learning what behaviors we have that enable our children to remain addicts, we can hope to shorten the duration of their addiction. Both of the family therapists in *Hope Never Lost* observed that parents spend their energy doing the wrong things out of ignorance. It is to every parent's benefit to learn from the experience of other parents who have lived with their child's addiction. We mothers in this book all found effective ways of coping with this challenge. We all learned how to keep our serenity and health even when our children did not choose recovery. We learned how to love our children in a way that would seem foreign to another parent. We feel it is helpful for parents to get the support offered by twelve-step programs in order to make the changes necessary to help both their child and themselves.

Through sharing our journeys and individual reflections on what had to change within us, in order for us to affect change in our children, we hope you will acquire a new perspective and gain the tools to endure the life-threatening progression you may be witnessing in your child.

We five mothers who shared our journeys raised our children in the suburbs of Pittsburgh and continue to reside in western Pennsylvania. Our ages range from fifty to sixty-five. In the midst of our child's addiction, we exhausted every avenue for support and guidance, which included the search for books relating to addiction in young adults. We were unable to find a book written by parents, for other parents, who were sharing the same experience. *Hope Never Lost* is the result of our desire to fill that void. We had all come to realize we were are no longer alone and that through sharing our experiences we learned so much from one another. Our individual journeys are far from over. With addiction comes much uncertainty. Our fears from the past can be easily triggered, and there are still days when our anxiety and despair resurface. In most cases our children are still overcoming the serious consequences from their years of addiction and struggle with the complexities of starting a new life without a chemical cushion.

We mothers have learned to find our strength when fear and sadness takes over, and to know when to step back and open our box of tools. It is at these times that our hope may be questioned or diminished but never lost.

Jay's mother speaks for the five of us when she says the following so well: When we look back over these years, we can say with confidence that it was not just one thing that brought us to our current understanding. God, Al-Anon, group therapy, our therapists, our sponsors, our faith traditions, love and prayers from family and friends, and all those who shared their experience, strength, and hope with us moved us to the place we are today. Once we opened our lives to individuals who understood addiction, our lives began to change. Once we opened our hearts to understanding addiction, things changed. Once we gave up thinking we could control our child, things changed. Once we gave up believing it was our fault, things changed. Once we accepted that our children had a chronic disease and that they could die if they did not take care of themselves, things changed. Once we accepted it was their choice to be in recovery, things changed. Once we accepted we needed to change some of our behaviors, we began to feel better. Once we accepted that God would take care of our children and loved them just as much as we did, things changed. We got out of God's way. We let our children take responsibility for their lives. We walked in faith and learned how to take care of ourselves first, and as we did that, we felt better. We felt more peace with our daily decisions. We began to trust our feelings and gained the hope we live with today.

ABOUT SOS

THE SUNLIGHT OF THE Spirit, SOS, was formed as a nonprofit family program of education and skill development for family members of individuals who suffer from the disease of chemical dependence. It was established in January of 2005. The three individuals who formed it understood that treating the entire family is crucial for two reasons: the family system becomes dysfunctional as a direct result of the disease of addiction, and the proper family responses can significantly increase the chances of recovery for the entire family.

From 1965 to 1985, a period often referred to as the "Camelot period," a number of leading institutions pioneered the treatment of the family—usually in a five-day residential program—while the addict or alcoholic was participating in his or her own treatment. Some of the most well-known programs were available at Johns

Hopkins Hospital, Sandstone Hospital, and Hazelden. However, with the advent of managed care, this focus on family treatment diminished. Unfortunately, since insurance pays only for the alcoholic or addict, not for the family, such programs are rare and most often self pay.

SOS was formed from the personal experiences and limitless commitment of its founders, a mother whose son was struggling with addiction, an addictions counselor, and a physician. All three completed their respective "professionals in residence" training at Hazelden and the Betty Ford Center. This training allowed the SOS founders to observe and absorb the concepts and activities used in the programs at these renowned treatment centers. They were determined to make life-changing family benefits available to family members of alcoholics and addicts in Western Pennsylvania.

AFTERWORD

IT IS DECEMBER 14, 2012, and one of the headlines in today's *Pittsburgh Post Gazette* reads, "Heroin: A Growing Addiction in Allegheny County." It states that heroin addiction is "a disease claiming the lives of our youth," and continues:

> An area medical director said it is the leading cause of accidental deaths in Allegheny County and most counties in western Pennsylvania.
> "In Allegheny County we set a record last year (with) 261 drug overdose deaths. That's more than traffic fatalities and homicides put together," said Dr. Neil Capretto, Medical Director at Gateway Rehabilitation Center...

The drug has punched its way from being an inner-city drug to being easily accessible in Pittsburgh's surrounding suburbs…

[Dr.] Capretto said more heroin is being used in western Pennsylvania right now than any other time in its history.

"It (heroin) is everywhere," he said. "It's very much become a middle- and upper-middle-class substance."

The article goes on to say that drug overdose deaths in the past ten years tripled among the county residents twenty-four years old and younger. In our small community paper alone, there is a listing in the obituaries at least once a month of someone under the age of twenty-five.

The five mothers in *Hope Never Lost* come from five different suburbs and are representative of just about any suburb in any city in the United States. It was not the neighborhood, school district or geographical area that led our children to drugs but rather the availability and opportunity to use so many different substances at such a young age. They chose to take a risk that led them down a path from which they could not escape.

No location in our country is immune from this growing disease. The harsh reality with which we live is drug abuse among our youth is an epidemic with no boundaries. It continues to spread among our younger generation at an age when many feel exempt from any risk. As a result they often lose their lives unintentionally while others choose to overdose as their only means of escaping this pernicious illness.

We all share hope in our society's ability to one day halt this progression, but until it does parents suffering from its profound effects must continue to seek help for themselves and derive support from one another.

selflessness
integrity
optimism
& leadership

Printed in Great Britain
by Amazon.co.uk, Ltd.,
Marston Gate.